BLOOMSBURY
CURRICULUM BASICS

Teaching Primary French

BLOOMSBURY CURRICULUM BASICS

Teaching Primary French

By Amanda Barton and Angela McLachlan

B L O O M S B U R Y

LONDON · OXFORD · NEW YORK · NEW DELHI · SYDNEY

Bloomsbury Education
An imprint of Bloomsbury Publishing Plc

50 Bedford Square	1385 Broadway
London	New York
WC1B 3DP	NY 10018
UK	USA

www.bloomsbury.com

Bloomsbury is a registered trademark of Bloomsbury Publishing Plc

First published 2016

British Library Cataloguing-in-Publication Data
A catalogue record for this book is available from the British Library.

ISBN:
PB 978-1-4729-2068-3
ePub 978-1-4729-2070-6
ePDF 978-1-4729-2069-0

Library of Congress Cataloging-in-Publication Data
A catalog record for this book is available from the Library of Congress.

10 9 8 7 6 5 4 3 2 1

Typeset by NewGen Knowledge Works (P) Ltd., Chennai, India
Printed and bound in Great Britain by CPI Group (UK) Ltd, Croydon CR0 4YY

This book is produced using paper that is made from wood grown in managed, sustainable
forests. It is natural, renewable and recyclable. The logging and manufacturing processes
conform to the environmental regulations of the country of origin.

To view more of our titles please visit www.bloomsbury.com

Other titles in the Bloomsbury Curriculum Basics series:

Teaching Primary History by Matthew Howorth

Teaching Primary Science by Peter Riley

Teaching Primary Spanish by Amanda Barton and Angela McLachlan

Teaching Primary Computing by Martin Burrett

Table of Contents

Introduction

Overview

This book sets out to equip readers with an understanding of how they can best teach children to make progress in French, the most widely taught language in primary schools. Intended for practitioners who are teaching or about to start teaching French at Key Stage 2 (KS2), it aims to boost confidence and enrich teachers' knowledge of the language. While it has been written primarily for those who do not specialise in the subject, practitioners with enhanced skills in French will also find the range of lesson plans extremely informative and useful.

Each chapter contains three easy-to-follow, step-by-step lesson plans that include all the French you need to know to cover the entire topic area, as well as all the French that pupils will learn in each individual lesson. We have selected the most common and primary-friendly topics, which range from broader areas such as numbers and weather, to looking more closely at the country and culture of France and French-speaking countries.

A list of resources required for each lesson is included, and activities are cross-referenced against the National Curriculum Programme of Study. Suggestions for further learning opportunities and cross-curricular activities follow each 30-minute lesson plan. The plans also provide guidance on pronunciation, and compare the French taught in the topics with the relevant English structures – these are often quite different, which can cause confusion for learners.

Given the challenges that schools and practitioners may face through the introduction of languages into the compulsory KS2 curriculum, we offer suggestions throughout the book for integrating French meaningfully into the primary school timetable, with particular support for those who do not specialise in teaching the language.

Recent developments in curriculum policy for primary languages

Languages became a statutory element of the KS2 curriculum in England in September 2014, bringing the English curriculum more in line with neighbouring European countries where languages are routinely taught from the age of six or seven. Languages also feature prominently in the primary curriculum in Scotland and Wales, and to a lesser extent in Northern Ireland.

State-maintained schools in England are now required to provide a structured programme of foreign language learning from Year 3 to Year 6. There is no preferred language: schools may select the language they wish to offer, and this may be a 'modern' language, such as French, German or Spanish, or an 'ancient' language, such as Latin, Hebrew or Greek.

The National Curriculum Programme of Study stipulates that schools should 'enable pupils to make substantial progress in one language', and while there should be a focus on one language in particular, the study of additional languages is not precluded. Giving pupils a taster of a range of languages can be effective in raising pupils' awareness of their own language, thereby fulfilling the Programme's requirement to 'lay the foundations for further foreign language teaching at Key Stage 3'. (DFE, 2013.)

The promotion of primary languages in England has run in parallel with a shift in the status of languages in secondary schools. Following the publication of the National Languages Strategy (DfES, 2002), the study of a language was removed from the compulsory KS4 curriculum, and was introduced as an 'entitlement' at KS2. The onus was thus switched from the later stages of secondary school to primary school, in the hope that motivating children at an early age to learn languages would inspire them to continue studying by choice at GCSE level.

The majority of primary schools now incorporate some language teaching in their curriculum; of the primary schools that responded to the annual 'Language Trends' survey in 2014, 99% were already teaching a language, and 12% began to teach a language in 2014. However, the survey revealed that schools are struggling with issues such as finding sufficient curriculum time, boosting the confidence of staff to teach languages, and increasing the linguistic competence of staff.

Why teach French at KS2?

Children are most motivated to learn when they are taught by a motivated teacher, and this is all the more so in a subject that is often considered 'difficult', as well as entirely new, to many pupils and practitioners. So it is worth considering what value you think teaching French really has, and what you hope you yourself, as well as your pupils, will gain from it. Below is a list of the potential benefits of teaching French to primary-aged children:

- The 'critical age theory' suggests that young children are much more adept at learning a language before they reach puberty; after this point, their linguistic capacity gradually diminishes. At this young age, children have fewer of the inhibitions that can impede their progress in adolescence, and are able to mimic pronunciation more accurately.
- Learning a language helps children develop their skills in listening, speaking, reading and writing, on which there is a particular emphasis in the Programme of Study for English at KS1 and 2. Pupils develop communication strategies that can be applied in their everyday lives, not just when speaking a foreign language. Learning is highly interactive and children spend more time speaking and listening in language lessons than in other subject areas. This can benefit children with special educational needs who may struggle with other curriculum areas.
- There are natural links with other curriculum areas, not least with literacy; these are highlighted in the lesson plans in this book.
- Teaching a foreign language offers a wealth of creative opportunities. Children are engaged in their learning through drama, singing, poetry, games and kinaesthetic activities that make language learning fun and exciting. Children often cite learning a foreign language as their favourite lesson in primary school.

- Understanding how people live and communicate in other countries and communities is enhanced through language learning. It can play an important role in raising awareness of other cultures and communities; this can be equally valuable whether you are teaching in a school with a diverse ethnic population or in a predominantly white, English-speaking community.

Why learn French in particular? This is a question that you might like to discuss with your pupils, especially when they are in Year 5 and 6. Pupils' response to this question is usually 'For going on holiday', but there are lots of other reasons, some of which are related to the usefulness of the language in pupils' long-term futures:

- Over 110 million people use French as their first language and 60 million people speak French as a second language.
- French is spoken in 54 countries around the world including Belgium, Canada, Switzerland, Madagascar, Haiti, Niger, Luxembourg, Morocco, Tunisia and Egypt. It is spoken on all five continents. (Chapter 2 looks at this in detail.)
- French is one of the most widely spoken languages in business and diplomacy.
- French speakers are always in demand from employers; language graduates have one of the lowest levels of unemployment after leaving university.
- French is the most popular language in secondary schools; learning French in primary school can therefore give pupils a significant head start.
- The English language contains many words derived from French.

Key whole-school issues in planning for primary French

- **How frequently should French be taught?**
  There are no formal requirements regarding timetabled French lessons. Nonetheless, everything we know about how children best learn a second or subsequent language in a classroom environment tells us that frequent opportunities to work with that language are essential. A weekly timetabled 'slot' for French, complemented by short 'encounters' with French during the school day, such as greetings, quick number or letter games, singing a song and so on, will enable pupils to progress successfully.

- **How regularly should French be taught?**
  Regular opportunities to learn French will result in enhanced learning outcomes. Primary schools generally have a busy 'whole-school' calendar, and often French is postponed in favour of other activities, or even removed from the timetable for a half or whole term. In the context of progression in language learning, lack of continuity can have a serious negative impact. The best model for learning French is a minimum of one lesson per week throughout the school year.

- **How long should a French lesson be?**
  Ideally, each individual lesson in Year 3 should be a minimum of 30 minutes, increasing to a minimum of 45 minutes by Year 6. Each lesson needs to include a review of the previous lesson, as well as opportunities for pupils to engage with language they have already worked with, across a blend of skills. In this book, the lesson plans vary between 30 and 45 minutes.

- **What should a French lesson cover?**
  Every French lesson should provide pupils with opportunities to revisit and practise language covered previously, in a variety of ways. It is not necessary – and can indeed be counterproductive – to introduce new language or a new concept in every lesson. The Programme of Study requires pupils to develop competence in the four skills of listening, speaking, reading and writing, and whilst 'isolating' skills in language learning is not advisable, focusing on particular skills at particular times works very well in terms of progress. If you are introducing new language in a lesson, keep the amount of new

content manageable, and ensure that it is situated in a communicative context that will allow pupils to use the language for practical communication. For example, with numbers 0–12, talking about the date today, or birthdays, provides pupils with a range of opportunities to apply their French across all four skills. This means teaching the months of the year alongside the numbers, as well as question formats. Chapter 4 includes lesson plans on this topic.

Lessons should regularly include cultural input, which allows pupils to develop their understanding of French and francophone (French-speaking) culture gradually, ideally complemented by opportunities to compare life in France with life in their home country. It is advisable to identify cross-curricular correspondences, as this will facilitate learning not only in French but in other subjects too. For instance, learning about the life cycle of a plant in science can be complemented by work on verbs, nouns and gender in French. The Norman Conquest in history allows you to study the impact this had on the English language in the words that the Normans left behind, as outlined in Chapter 1. In numeracy, recognising number patterns or practising times tables can be consolidated and enhanced by appropriate activities in French, as outlined in Chapter 4.

- **Should I give French homework?**
  Each school has its own homework policy, often focusing on developing literacy and numeracy skills. Crafted appropriately, French homework can contribute to the development of these wider skills, in addition to pupils' progress in French.

Introduction to the KS2 Programme of Study for Languages

The Programme of Study for Languages is unique in that, unlike other curriculum areas, it does not prescribe content across individual year groups. The focus is predominantly on the development of generic skills in listening, speaking, reading and writing, with significant alignment with the aims and objectives of the Programme of Study for English. We can see here explicit correspondences with the Programme of Study for Languages at KS3, as well as with the specifications for GCSE languages examinations offered by all four awarding bodies in England (AQA, Edexcel, Eduqas and OCR), where each skill now has an equal weighting of 25%.

Additionally, there is no specific national attainment standard, either by year group or by the end of KS2. Planning carefully longer term to ensure progression in learning is therefore essential.

Table 1.1 shows the scope of what pupils should learn in French in KS2 in all four skill areas. *Italics* indicate key implications for practice.

Table 1.1 Overview of Programme of Study for Languages at KS2

Programme of Study for Languages	
Purpose of study	Learning a foreign language is a liberation from insularity and *provides an opening to other cultures.* A high-quality languages education should foster pupils' curiosity and deepen their understanding of the world. *The teaching should enable pupils to express their ideas and thoughts in another language and to understand and respond to its speakers, both in speech and in writing.* It should also provide opportunities for them to *communicate for practical purposes,* learn new ways of thinking and read great literature in the original language. Language teaching should provide the foundation for learning further languages, equipping pupils to study and work in other countries.

Aims: to ensure that all pupils…	understand and respond to spoken and written language *from a variety of authentic sources*	*speak with increasing confidence, fluency and spontaneity*, finding ways of communicating what they want to say, including through discussion and asking questions, and continually improving the *accuracy of their pronunciation and intonation*	*can write at varying length, for different purposes and audiences, using the variety of grammatical structures that they have learnt*	*discover and develop an appreciation of a range of writing in the language studied*
Skills focus	*listen attentively* to spoken language and show understanding by joining in and responding	*speak in sentences*, using familiar vocabulary, phrases and basic language structures	*read carefully* and show understanding of words, phrases and simple writing	*write* phrases from memory, and adapt these to create new sentences, to express ideas clearly
Learning in the classroom	explore the patterns and sounds of language through songs and rhymes and link the spelling, sound and meaning of words engage in conversations; ask *and answer* questions; express opinions *and respond to* those of others; seek clarification and help appreciate stories, songs, poems and rhymes in the language	engage in conversation; ask and answer questions; express opinions and respond to those of others; seek clarification and help develop accurate pronunciation and intonation so that others understand when they are using familiar words and phrases present ideas and information orally to a range of audiences describe people, places, things and actions orally	appreciate stories, songs, poems and rhymes in the language broaden their vocabulary and develop their ability to understand new words that are introduced into familiar written material, including through using a dictionary develop accurate pronunciation and intonation so that others understand when they are reading aloud	describe people, places, things and actions in writing
Conceptual knowledge	Understand basic grammar appropriate to the language being studied, including (where relevant): feminine, masculine and neuter forms and the conjugation of high-frequency verbs; key features and patterns of the language; how to apply these, for instance, to build sentences; and how these differ from or are similar to English.			
Assessment & measuring progress	By the end of each Key Stage, pupils are expected to know, apply and understand the matters, skills and processes specified in the relevant programme of study.			

Source: DFE-00174–2013, Crown Copyright, 2013

The Programme of Study for Languages at KS2 can be downloaded in full from: www.gov.uk/government/uploads/system/uploads/attachment_data/file/239042/PRIMARY_national_curriculum_-_Languages.pdf

In the context of progression and continuity in learning, you will also find it useful to familiarise yourself with the Programme of Study for Languages at KS3, which is available at: www.gov.uk/government/uploads/system/uploads/attachment_data/file/239083/SECONDARY_national_curriculum_-_Languages.pdf

The learner perspective: what do pupils say about primary French?

We asked a number of KS2 pupils to tell us about their languages lessons, and to think about what a 'good' primary languages lesson is like. Their responses can meaningfully inform our planning for successful learning.

I think a good lesson is:
- Where we do active things, not just copying from the board or doing exercises in the book. (**Yr 6 pupil**)
- Where we don't have to learn loads of words on their own, because you forget them really quickly. (**Yr 6 pupil**)
- Where we don't just do loads of games or PowerPoints coz we get PowerPoints all the time. (**Yr 6 pupil**)
- One where we can learn more about [France] as a country, things like its history, or what young people do, what they eat and if they have to do SATs. (**Yr 6 pupil**)
- Where we can play games to help us remember things, and then have a go at saying them ourselves. (**Yr 5 pupil**)

What I like about my languages lessons:
- I like doing the songs and things, but I don't really like a lot of copying or labelling things. I think languages are important, though, because it shows you're clever enough to try to understand other countries. (**Yr 5 pupil**)
- I like the lessons, but not when we have to wait ages for everyone to finish the work coz it's boring. (**Yr 4 pupil**)
- I like to know why things are different and stuff, so I like it when we do grammar with all the rules and things, then I can do it on my own, but I don't think everyone likes it. (**Yr 6 pupil**)
- I don't like it when we have to miss French for something, because I can't remember what we did last time, and it's like you have to start all over again. (**Yr 4 pupil**)

Overview of the French you will need for KS2

As we have already discussed, the Programme of Study for Languages at KS2 does not prescribe specific content to be taught and learnt in primary French. However, a programme including any or all of the following areas of vocabulary, topics/themes and grammatical input is generally accepted to be the most appropriate and relevant for primary pupils. Teachers can map content and concepts across individual year groups, according to their own particular school context. We have also identified subjects in which there is opportunity for cross-curricular learning.

Vocabulary and language

- High-frequency adjectives, including colours (literacy, English, science)
- Alphabet (literacy, English)

- Animals (science)
- At home (literacy, English)
- Classroom language and objects (practical communication in French)
- Clothing (literacy, English, science)
- Countries, capitals, continents (geography)
- Daily routine (literacy, English)
- Days of the week, months and seasons of the year (practical communication in French, science)
- Directions and compass points (practical communication in French, science, geography)
- Family (literacy, English)
- Food and drink (science, healthy eating)
- Fruits and vegetables (science, healthy eating, numeracy)
- Greetings and praise (practical communication in French)
- Health and illness (science)
- In town, including buildings, shops and public areas
- Musical instruments
- Cardinal numbers, minimum 0–100 (numeracy)
- Ordinal numbers, minimum 1st–3rd (numeracy)
- Parts of the body (science)
- Planets and space (science)
- School subjects (practical communication in French)
- Shapes and angles (numeracy, maths)
- Sports (PE)
- Telling the time (practical communication in French, numeracy)
- Transport (geography)
- Weather (science)

Grammatical concepts

- Adjectival agreement and position
- Adverbs
- Comparisons and superlatives
- Connectives and conjunctions
- Definite, indefinite and partitive articles
- Elision
- Expressing opinions
- Gender
- High-frequency verbs with some reference to conjugation
- Interrogative pronouns
- Possessive adjectives
- Question formats
- Negatives
- Personal pronouns
- Punctuation
- Prepositions
- Singular and plural forms of nouns
- Tense: competence in recognising and using the present tense accurately as a minimum, some reference to the conjugation of future and past tenses desirable

Phonological awareness

- Basic understanding of French phonics, and similarities with/differences to the English sound system
- Developing confidence and competence in pronunciation, based on phonological awareness

Cultural knowledge and understanding

- Architects (art and design, science, geography, history)
- Art and artists, including photographers and sculptors (art and design)
- Athletes and sports-people (PE, science)
- Composers (music)
- The francophone world (geography, history)
- Historical timelines (history, geography, RE)
- National and regional festivals and traditions (RE, geography)
- Films (history, geography, RE)
- Foods (science, geography, literacy, English)
- Historical and political figures (history, RE, geography, general knowledge)
- Landmarks and monuments (geography, general knowledge)
- Musicians and singers (music)
- Scientists (science)
- The topography of France and francophone countries (geography)
- Writers, playwrights and poets (literacy, English)

Developing your subject knowledge in French

Primary practitioners require a sound baseline competence in French in order to be able to teach it effectively. It is important that you use as much spoken French language as possible in the classroom in order to promote pupils' speaking and listening skills. Chapter 1 outlines some basic classroom instructions that can become part of a regular classroom routine.

As the practitioner, you are providing the main model of spoken language, therefore it is crucial that pronunciation is accurate. In some sections of the book we have identified websites that you can visit to check your pronunciation of the vocabulary being taught in the lesson. It is also worth looking at www.lightbulblanguages.co.uk/resources/audio/ where you can download podcasts.

As you prepare to teach, it is a good idea to audit your French subject knowledge, and on the basis of that, map out a realistic and achievable action plan to refresh or develop your French skills. Start by reviewing the list of the French you are likely to need across KS2 above, then answer the following questions:

1. To what extent are my French language skills sufficient to enable me to support progression in pupil learning successfully?
2. What strategies could I adopt to improve my knowledge base in French in order to support language teaching and learning successfully?
3. What does it feel like to be a language learner, and what are the implications for teaching and learning in the primary French classroom?

You might also find it useful to audit your skills against the *Common European Framework of Reference for Languages*, or CEFR. Initially developed by the Council for Europe some 30 years ago to promote across Europe a shared understanding of language competence, it suggests attainment descriptors for language learners across six core levels. These levels, illustrated in Table 1.2, are mapped across three distinct phases – *basic user, independent user* and *proficient user* – and provide a useful development plan for practitioners.

Table 1.2 CEFR Common Reference Levels

Proficient User	C2	Can understand with ease virtually everything heard or read. Can summarise information from different spoken and written sources, reconstructing arguments and accounts in a coherent presentation. Can express him/herself spontaneously, very fluently and precisely, differentiating finer shades of meaning even in more complex situations.
	C1	Can understand a wide range of demanding, longer texts, and recognise implicit meaning. Can express him/herself fluently and spontaneously without much obvious searching for expressions. Can use language flexibly and effectively for social, academic and professional purposes. Can produce clear, well-structured, detailed text on complex subjects, showing controlled use of organisational patterns, connectors and cohesive devices.
Independent User	B2	Can understand the main ideas of complex text on both concrete and abstract topics, including technical discussions in his/her field of specialisation. Can interact with a degree of fluency and spontaneity that makes regular interaction with native speakers quite possible without strain for either party. Can produce clear, detailed text on a wide range of subjects and explain a viewpoint on a topical issue giving the advantages and disadvantages of various options.
	B1	Can understand the main points of clear standard input on familiar matters regularly encountered in work, school, leisure, etc. Can deal with most situations likely to arise whilst travelling in an area where the language is spoken. Can produce simple connected text on topics which are familiar or of personal interest. Can describe experiences and events, dreams, hopes and ambitions and briefly give reasons and explanations for opinions and plans.
Basic User	A2	Can understand sentences and frequently used expressions related to areas of most immediate relevance (e.g. very basic personal and family information, shopping, local geography, employment). Can communicate in simple and routine tasks requiring a simple and direct exchange of information on familiar and routine matters. Can describe in simple terms aspects of his/her background, immediate environment **and** matters in areas of immediate need.
	A1	Can understand and use familiar everyday expressions and very basic phrases aimed at the satisfaction of needs of a concrete type. Can introduce him/herself and others and can ask and answer questions about personal details such as where he/she lives, people he/she knows and things he/she has. Can interact in a simple way provided the other person talks slowly and clearly and is prepared to help.

Source: www.coe.int/t/dg4/linguistic/source/framework_En.pdf

Consider the following as you begin to develop or refresh your French:

- Be realistic about *when*: teachers lead very busy lives, so it's useful to map out in advance particular days when you can work on your French.
- *Little and often* works best in language learning, rather than 'big chunks' at infrequent intervals.
- Think about *how* you will work on your French: a self-access course, night school, online, for example? Do you have a colleague or friend you can learn with? This is particularly useful for listening and speaking practice. Have a look at *Teach Yourself French for Primary School Teachers* (McLachlan, 2010, Hodder Education); the book focuses on the range of French you are likely to need across KS2.
- *Watch and listen*: do you know any schools where French is taught? Spend some time observing lessons across KS2: this will enhance both your subject knowledge and your understanding of subject-specific pedagogy.

- Avoid learning large banks of individual words without putting them in a communicative context: knowing lots of single words does not give you any opportunity to actually use them.
- *Think French*: create a space in your classroom that is entirely French (label items, display frequently used language and so on); select a French website as your whiteboard/laptop/tablet homepage; play audio materials as often as you can at home, when travelling, during break time at school, for example – this is particularly useful for listening and pronunciation.
- *Use your French*: try to use your French as often as possible, particularly at school – pupils will soon begin to greet you in French too.
- *Invest in a bilingual dictionary*: there are several excellent beginners' French-English bilingual dictionaries; use one that you can also use with your pupils, rather than a more 'advanced' one, for example the *Collins First Time* or *Easy Learning French* dictionary, or the *Oxford First Learner's French Dictionary*.
- *Set goals* and *keep track of your progress*: simply transfer the principles of learning from your classroom to your French – it really does work!
- Take some time to browse around the extensive Languages area at www.bbc.co.uk/languages/, and check your progress on the GCSE Bitesize pages.
- Visit Language World, the annual conference of the Association for Language Learning (ALL), the UK's largest professional body for all teachers of languages. This offers the biggest exhibition of language teaching materials in the country (which is free to visit) and a vast array of workshops to choose from. Discounted entry is available to members; see www.all-languages.org.uk/about/what_can_all_do_for_me/I_am_a_primary_teacher for details of membership and what ALL offers, including online resources, local support networks and regional workshops.

Lesson plans

The exemplar lesson plans are designed for 30-minute lessons, suitable for any year group. Practitioners will be able to adapt activities according to the context of their particular class, for example age, ability level, prior experience of learning languages and time available to teach French.

Successful teaching and learning in languages relies on a meaningful blend of skills work, and each plan includes multi-skill activities, combining listening, speaking, reading and writing. Each chapter addresses a particular topic and the plans are structured in the same way, addressing a specific range of language, and including the following sections:

- What does the curriculum say?
- What do I need to know?
- The French you need to teach these lessons
- Comparing English with French
- Three exemplar lesson plans
- Cross-curricular links
- Further learning opportunities.

References

DFE (2013) National Curriculum in England: languages programme of study
CfBT Education Trust (2015) 'Language Trends 2014/15: The state of language learning in primary and secondary schools in England'
National Languages Strategy (2002) 'Languages for All: Languages for Life', DfES Publications

1 *Allons-y!* Getting started

What does the curriculum say?

- *Learning a foreign language is a liberation from insularity and provides an opening to other cultures. A high-quality languages education should foster pupils' curiosity and deepen their understanding of the world.*
- *The teaching should provide an appropriate balance of spoken and written language and should lay the foundations for further foreign language teaching at KS3.*

Pupils should be taught to:
- *Listen attentively to spoken language and show understanding by joining in and responding.*
- *Read carefully and show understanding of words, phrases and simple writing.*

What do I need to know?

This chapter is about setting the context for learning French in the primary classroom. The first lesson plan sets up the classroom as a French-speaking environment. The second lesson sets out the broader cultural context and encourages pupils to consider why learning foreign languages is important. The third aims to boost children's confidence and shows how they can draw on knowledge and skills they already have when learning a new language.

Lesson 1 does not require the children to speak any French. The focus is simply on the pupils listening and responding, attuning them to the sounds of French and preparing them to be able to respond to basic classroom instructions.

Lesson 2 increases pupils' awareness of the need to learn languages other than English, by exploring how many languages are spoken in the world and in which countries. It explodes some of the myths that children have about the predominance of English.

Lesson 3 demonstrates to pupils that they already have a range of strategies at their disposal that will help them to understand and learn French.

Comparing English with French

- The classroom instructions in Lesson 1 are all in the formal imperative form, i.e. the *vous* form of the verb, which is used when addressing more than one person or to convey respect.
- *En anglais*: French uses a lower-case letter for languages, in contrast to English.
- The acute accent in *écoutez* and *répétez* changes the sound of the 'e' to 'ay'. The -ez ending on *répétez*, *trouvez*, *levez* and *asseyez* also sounds like 'ay'.
- The -*i* ending on *qui* and *fini* is pronounced as 'ee'.

- *Levez-vous* and *asseyez-vous* both derive from reflexive verbs, hence the additional *vous* pronoun. This is the equivalent of saying 'stand yourself up' or 'sit yourself down' in English.
- In the paragraph to be read aloud in Lesson 3, *fils* (son) is pronounced as 'feese' and *fille* as 'fee'. French does not pronounce the 'h' as in English, hence *j'habite* is pronounced as 'j'abite' and *hamster* as 'amstaire'.

The French you need to teach these lessons

- 10 basic classroom instructions (see Lesson 1)
- The phrase *Jacques a dit* ('Simon says')
- Secure pronunciation and understanding of the paragraph used at the beginning of Lesson 3

Lesson 1 Basic classroom language

Objectives and outcomes
Today we will:
- Learn some French that you're going to hear a lot in French lessons.

French to be learned by pupils
Silence! Silence!
Trouvez la page ... Find page ...
Qui n'a pas fini? Who hasn't finished?
En anglais? In English?
Écoutez Listen
Répétez Repeat after me
Travaillez à deux Work in pairs
Levez-vous Stand up
Asseyez-vous Sit down
Très bien Very good

Resources you will need
- 10 A4 cards, each displaying one of the classroom instructions
- Blu-Tack for sticking the instruction cards to the walls

Getting started
5 minutes
- Explain in English that pupils are going to learn some phrases that you'll be using regularly in future lessons.
- Read through the list of French phrases and ask pupils to guess the meanings in English, listening out for similarities with English. (The phrases are listed above and below in order of accessibility, with those most difficult to access towards the bottom of the list.)

Class activities

20 minutes

- Read out each of the phrases in French and accompany each one with an action for the class to copy:

    Silence – fingers on lips

    Trouvez la page ... – turn the pages of a book

    Qui n'a pas fini? – 'stop' sign with one hand

    En anglais? – both hands in a querying gesture

    Écoutez – hands cupping your ears

    Répétez – point to your mouth, then point to the class

    Travaillez à deux – point to two pupils, one at a time

    Levez-vous – stand up

    Asseyez-vous – sit down

    Très bien – thumbs up

You may want to invite the class to make their own suggestions for memorable actions.

- Repeat the phrases and actions several times, varying the order in which you say them, and at an increasing pace.
- Repeat the phrases but do not perform the action. Pupils perform the action.
- Play a game of '*Jacques a dit*' ('Simon says') in French. Insert (or deliberately omit) *Jacques a dit* before each instruction. Pupils who perform the action when *Jacques a dit* does not precede the instruction are out.

Plenary

5 minutes

- Show the pupils the instructions displayed on pieces of card and ask them to read them aloud as a class.
- Hand over each card to a pupil and ask each pupil to stick their card somewhere around the room.
- Read out the phrases and ask pupils to point to the card displaying that phrase.

Lesson 2 Why learn languages?

Objectives and outcomes

Today we will:

- Think about how many different languages are spoken in the world, and why it's so important to learn other languages.

Resources you will need

- 8 A4 cards displaying a language on one side and the number of speakers and countries where the language is spoken on the reverse, as outlined in **Bloomsbury Online Resource 1A**
- Pre-researched answers to questions 4 and 5 in the starter activity

Getting started

10 minutes

- Ask pupils to answer the following questions, either in groups, then feeding back to the whole class, or as a whole class:

  1. How many languages can you think of?
  2. How many languages do you speak?
  3. How many languages are spoken on your table?
  4. How many languages are spoken in your class?
  5. How many languages do you think are spoken in this school?
  6. How many languages do you think are spoken in the UK?
  7. Have you ever spoken a foreign language?

- Discuss the responses as a whole class and provide the answers to questions 4, 5 and 6 (around 100 languages are spoken in the UK.)

Class activities

15 minutes

- Which are the world's most widely spoken languages? Ask the class which languages they think are most widely spoken in the world.
- Invite eight pupils to the front of the class and hand each of them a card. On the front of the card is the name of a language, and on the reverse – visible only to the individual pupil holding the card – is the number of people in the world who speak that language, together with a list of some of the countries where the language is spoken.
- The pupils stand in a line in front of the class, displaying only the language on their cards, and the rest of the class work together to arrange the pupils in a line, with the most widely spoken language furthest to their left and the eighth most widely spoken language to their right.
- Once a consensus has been reached by the class, the cardholders take it in turn to read out how many people in the world speak the language on their card, and the class rearrange the cards accordingly; this is an excellent exercise in numeracy.
- Ask the rest of the class to name some of the countries in which they think those languages are spoken. Each cardholder then reads out the countries on the back of his or her card. See **Bloomsbury Online Resource 1A** for the information to display on pupils' cards.

Plenary

5 minutes

- Highlight the position of 'English' in the ranking. Ask pupils to come up with as many reasons as possible as to why it is a good idea to learn other languages. The answers could be incorporated in a display.

Lesson 3 Being a language detective

Objectives and outcomes

Today we will:

• Become language detectives.

Resources you will need

• A written copy of the paragraph used in the Starter activity, to read aloud
• Self-made worksheet for pupils, showing a range of texts in different languages – include texts such as a letter, a menu, a TV schedule, the weather forecast etc.

Getting started

5 minutes

• Inform pupils that you are going to read them part of an email that has just been sent to you by a teacher in France. They must try to understand as much as they can. Read the text aloud twice.
• Read out the following text in French only, using gestures to illustrate your points:

Je m'appelle Madame Rangier. J'habite dans un appartement à Paris. J'ai deux enfants: un grand fils qui s'appelle Alexandre et une petite fille qui s'appelle Amélie. Nous avons deux animaux: un hamster qui s'appelle Betty et un chat qui s'appelle Trixie.

'I am called Mrs. Rangier. I live in a flat in Paris. I have two children: a big son who is called Alexander and a little daughter called Amelie. We have two pets: a hamster called Betty and a cat called Trixie.'

• Ask pupils to tell you how much of the email they understand.
• Ask pupils to list the strategies they used to help them understand, for instance observing body language and actions, or listening to the names of people (proper nouns) and words that sound like English (we call these 'cognates').
• Point out that the pupils understand more French than they probably first realised, and that they can use this knowledge to help them in their future French lessons.

Class activities

20 minutes

• Show pupils a number of different types of text, e.g. letters, recipes, menus, adverts, a weather forecast, a TV schedule and school timetables. It does not matter what language or languages the texts are in; the objective is to train the pupils to look at the format of each text in order to infer what kind of text it is. This is an excellent literacy activity.
• As a challenge activity, ask pupils to identify the kind of writing exemplified in each text, together with any words they understand from English – these will likely be cognates. (see **Bloomsbury Online Resource 1B** for an example worksheet.)

Plenary

5 minutes

• Discuss the pupils' answers and the clues they used to help them understand the texts, e.g. pictures, layout of the text, measurements in a recipe or perhaps clock times in TV listings.

Cross-curricular links

RE: Read the story of the Tower of Babel to pupils and discuss why there are so many different languages.

History: Link with the Norman invasion by listing words that the English language borrows from the French, e.g. bouquet, café, chauffeur, chic, cul de sac, fiancé, omelette, restaurant.

Geography: Ask pupils to locate the countries mentioned in the 'World's most widely spoken languages' activity (Lesson 2) on a map.

PE: Do a basic warm-up/'Take 5' activity, with French instructions:

marchez walk
sautez jump
dansez dance
plus vite faster
plus lentement slower
arrêtez stop

Numeracy: As a written follow-up, and to consolidate the 'World's most widely-spoken languages' activity from Lesson 2, pupils complete **Bloomsbury Online Resource 1C**.

Further learning opportunities

- Reinforce the classroom instructions through regular use. It is important that pupils are exposed to as much spoken French language as possible.
- Add to the list of classroom instructions, including some that pupils will use themselves, to get them into the habit of using French to communicate spontaneously:

  Je ne comprends pas I don't understand
  Qui ne comprend pas? Who doesn't understand?
  Levez la main Put your hand up
  Fermez la porte Close the door
  Fermez les yeux Close your eyes
  Ouvrez les yeux Open your eyes
  Ouvrez les livres Open your books
  Rangez les affaires Pack your things away
  Écrivez Write it down
  Toute la classe The whole class
  Des volontaires? Any volunteers?
  Avec un partenaire With a partner (male)
  Avec une partenaire With a partner (female)

- Ask pupils to prepare a French folder in which to store their work. Encourage them to stick images of French places/people/words onto their folders.
- Set pupils the task of interviewing teachers/parents/family/friends to find out how many languages they can speak.
- Create a multilingual environment in your classroom by displaying posters showing the French words for classroom objects, such as 'door' and 'desk', as well as greetings in other languages.
- Ask pupils to find examples of foreign language text on the packaging of products, e.g. food packaging, and bring them into school. How much do they understand?
- The website www.language-investigator.co.uk aims to enhance pupils' language awareness, and contains a lot of information that can be downloaded as well as many useful links.

2 *Bonjour la France et la Francophonie!* Hello France and French-speaking countries!

What does the curriculum say?

Teachers should aim to:
- *Provide an opening to other cultures.*
- *Foster pupils' curiosity and deepen their understanding of the world.*

What do I need to know?

Exploring France and French-speaking countries provides pupils with a fabulous opportunity to develop their understanding of the wider world, and equally importantly, to contextualise the language they are learning by making French 'real'. It is useful to begin your French programme with a series of lessons that give pupils a flavour of France, and what is known as *la Francophonie* (French-speaking countries), and to continue throughout the school year with regular lessons focusing on cultural, geographical and social aspects of life in those countries. You may find that many children are not necessarily aware of their own immediate geographical environment, so it is important to explore your home town or city, and where it is located in England (or your home country), prior to introducing France, Europe and countries across the world in which French is spoken.

Lesson 1 introduces pupils to France and its location in Europe, with reference to the location of England (or your home country). It includes a range of 'fascinating facts' about France, the French language and French-speaking countries for them to discuss.

Lesson 2 explores Paris, looks at some of its most famous landmarks and monuments, and gives pupils an opportunity to write some words in French.

Lesson 3 looks beyond France, introduces pupils to *les pays francophones* – countries across the world where French is the official language – and gives them the opportunity to begin to read in French.

Comparing English with French

- As in English, countries in French are proper nouns, and are always written with a capital letter. Additionally, each country is either masculine or feminine, for example *la France*, *la Suisse*, *le Canada*.

- The definite article ('the') is abbreviated both in the masculine *(le)* and the feminine *(la)* if it comes before a noun beginning with a vowel. For example: *l'Ouganda* (Uganda, masculine), *l'Angleterre* (England, feminine), *l'Europe* (Europe, feminine).
- *Tour* has two meanings in French, determined by its gender: *la tour* means 'tower', as in *La Tour Eiffel*, and *le tour* means 'tour', as in *Le Tour de France*.
- In English, we use a capital/upper-case letter *(majuscule)* when talking about particular languages, for example: 'I speak English', 'I speak French', 'I speak Spanish'. In French, we use a small, or lower-case letter *(minuscule)*, for example: *Je parle anglais, Je parle français, Je parle espagnol*.

The French you need to teach these lessons

- *voici* here is/here are
- *c'est* this is/it is
- *la capitale de la/du/de l'* the capital of
- A range of capital cities, listed in Lesson 3
- *anglais* English
- *La Manche* the English Channel
- *le Tricolore: bleu, blanc, rouge* the French flag: blue, white, red
- *montrez-moi* show me
- *ici on parle français* French is spoken here
- A selection of French landmarks and monuments (see Lesson 1)
- Countries where French is spoken (given in individual lists within the relevant Lessons)

Lesson 1 *Bienvenue en France!* Welcome to France!

Objectives and outcomes
Today we will:
- Learn how to locate France and its capital city on a map of Europe.
- Learn some fascinating facts about France and French.
- Practise our French pronunciation.

French to be learned by pupils
anglais English
français French
l'Angleterre (or *l'Écosse, le Pays de Galles, l'Irlande du Nord*, depending on your home country)
Londres, Édimbourg, Cardiff, Belfast London, Edinburgh, Cardiff, Belfast
la France France
Paris Paris
le Tricolore the French flag
l'Europe Europe

Resources you will need
- Map of Europe, clearly showing where both France and England (or your home country) are located in Europe (or your home continent). The map should also show the English Channel – *La Manche*. (See **Bloomsbury Online Resource 2A**.)
- Laminated picture of the English flag, or other symbol to denote the use of English (See **Bloomsbury Online Resource 2B**).
- Laminated picture of the French flag, or other symbol to denote the use of French (See **Bloomsbury Online Resource 2C**).
- PowerPoint presentation, called *La France, c'est fascinant!* In your presentation you should include a picture of the French flag, called *le Tricolore* (literally 'three colours'), and between 10 and 20 'fascinating facts about France', depending on the age group of the pupils. (see the 'facts bank' at the bottom of this lesson for suggestions).

Getting started
5 minutes
- Hold up the laminated English flag/your chosen symbol to show that you will be using English for this exercise.
- Introduce objectives and outcomes, including learning plenary questions, for example:
  - What is your favourite fact about France that you learned today, and why?
  - Tell us one thing you'd most like to learn more about, and why.
- Initiate whole-group questioning (still in English), eliciting what pupils understand about the location of England (or your home country) within Europe (or your home continent), including reference to the capital and other major cities.
- Next, introduce whole-group questioning about France and French.
- You might like to try the 'snowball starter' if pupils are familiar with this, or use your French lessons to introduce them to it, and then use it in other curriculum areas. Pupils select a learning partner, and in 20 seconds share with each other everything they know about France, noting their facts either on a mini whiteboard or in their workbooks. Ring a bell or similar after 20 seconds, then the pairs walk around the room, sharing their facts with another pair,

comparing what they have, and adding any new facts to their own. After 3 minutes or so, have a whole-group fact-sharing discussion.

Class activities
20 minutes
- Hold up the laminated French flag/your chosen symbol to show that you will now be speaking French.
- Screen the map of Europe, saying *Voici l'Europe*.
- Pupils repeat the phrase several times; to check for understanding, ask *En anglais, c'est... ?* It is acceptable to repeat this in English if necessary at the very beginning, to ensure that they understand; in subsequent lessons you will not need to do this, as pupils will very quickly learn that you are asking 'What does this mean in English?'
- Now point to England (or your home country), saying *Voici l'Angleterre*, following the same procedure for repetition.
- Introduce the capital city, saying *Voici Londres, la capitale de l'Angleterre*; focus particularly on the 'r' sound.
- Pupils will also find it interesting to see where their home town or city is in relation to London.
- Now point out the location of France, saying *Voici la France!* Pupils repeat the phrase several times.
- Follow the same procedure with Paris, saying *Voici Paris, la capitale de la France*.
- To practise pronunciation of the words, carry out a brief Q&A, for example: *Oui ou non: Londres est la capitale de la France? Vrai ou faux: Paris est la capitale de l'Angleterre? C'est la France? C'est l'Angleterre?* Accepting simple, one-word answers encourages pupils to participate, and also enables you to evaluate children's understanding. Expecting all pupils to assimilate complete phrases such as *Paris est la capitale de la France* in a single lesson is not realistic.
- Point out the English Channel, saying *Voici la Manche!* It's useful to introduce this bilingually, and to discuss in English whether pupils have heard of the English Channel, the Channel Tunnel and so on.
- Hold up the laminated flag/symbol for English so that they understand that you will now be using English as the means of communication.
- Screen the presentation, focusing on the fascinating facts. Engaging pupils in discussion about each fact as you present it works really well. Make reference to any 'new' facts in your presentation that were not included in the whole-group starter activity.

Plenary
5 minutes
- Remind pupils of the objectives/outcomes and ask whether they have achieved the outcomes (e.g. thumbs up, thumbs down). You may like to create a set of three cards per child, showing *oui, non* and *un peu*, for them to convey their answers.
- Ask learning plenary questions and note responses to inform future planning, for example:
  - What is your favourite fact about France that you learned today, and why?
  - Tell us one thing you'd most like to learn more about, and why.

Facts bank
Wow words!
- Breakfast is called *le petit déjeuner* in French, which means 'little lunch'.
- *Bon appétit!* means 'Enjoy your meal!'
- *Miam-miam!* means 'yum yum!' in French.
- To wish someone a nice day, say *Bonne journée!*
- Pancake or Shrove Tuesday is called *Mardi Gras* in French. That means 'Fat Tuesday'!

Geography focus

- The French flag has three colours: blue, white and red, and is known as le *Tricolore*.
- France is the largest country in western Europe.
- France shares a border with eight other countries: Andorra, Belgium, Germany, Italy, Luxembourg, Monaco, Spain and Switzerland.
- The highest mountain in the French Alps is *Mont Blanc*, which is 4,810 metres high. *Mont Blanc* means 'White Mountain'.

Food focus

- A *baguette* is a very popular type of bread in France. It actually means 'little stick', because it looks like a stick of bread.
- Pupils might be familiar with the French cheeses *Camembert* and *Brie*. There are hundreds of different kinds of cheese in France!
- *Le chocolat chaud* means hot chocolate, and is often drunk at breakfast. It's usually served in a small bowl, rather than a cup.
- A *croque-monsieur* is a grilled ham and cheese sandwich, and is a very common item on French bistro and café menus.

Transport focus

- The Channel Tunnel links England and France, and is 34 miles long. Nearly 24 miles are actually under the English Channel: *La Manche*.
- You can get a train from London all the way to Paris. The train travels through the Channel Tunnel.
- *Le Métro* is the name for the famous underground railway system in Paris.
- You can travel around France very quickly on the *TGV*; this stands for *Train à Grande Vitesse*, which means 'high-speed train' in English.

Life in France

- The currency is the French euro, which is worth between 70 and 80 pence.
- When greeting friends in France, it is quite usual to kiss them on the cheek at least once.
- The French national anthem is called '*La Marseillaise*'.
- The *fleur de lys* (lily flower) is one of the national symbols of France.
- One of the most important dates in the French national calendar (and some would say *the* most important date!), is 14 July, *le quatorze juillet, la Fête Nationale française*, also known as *Le Jour de la Bastille*, Bastille Day.

Lesson 2 *Bienvenue à Paris!* Welcome to Paris!

Objectives and outcomes
Today we will:
- Explore the capital city of Paris.
- Write the name of some famous Parisian landmarks in French.

French to be learned by pupils
c'est this is/it is
voici here is/here are
la Tour Eiffel the Eiffel Tower
l'Arc de Triomphe the Triumph Arch
la Seine the River Seine
le Musée du Louvre the Louvre

Resources you will need
- PowerPoint presentation or similar, entitled *Bonjour Paris!*, with pictures of a range of Parisian landmarks and monuments, and the names written in both English and French. A selection of introductory landmarks is given below, although there are, of course, many more that you can research online, and may prefer to use.
- Reference sheet showing these landmarks/monuments; one per learning pair will be sufficient. Laminate these for repeated use. (See **Bloomsbury Online Resource 2D**).
- Worksheet with your selected Parisian landmarks/monuments for pupils to label. (See **Bloomsbury Online Resource 2E**).

Getting started
5 minutes
- Hold up the laminated flag/symbol for English, to show that you will be using English.
- Introduce the objectives and outcomes, including learning plenary questions, for example:
  - You have 60 seconds to tell us everything we learned about Paris today.
  - Tell us what you know now about Paris that you didn't know at the beginning of the lesson.
- Quick oral quiz based on the 'fascinating facts' you chose for Lesson 1.
- Quick oral vocab quiz asking, for example, *Londres en anglais? La France en anglais?* For increased challenge, ask *London en français? France en français?* You can also ask the question in a more complete form: *Comment dit-on la capitale en anglais? Comment dit-on La Manche en anglais?*

Class activities
20 minutes
- Screen your presentation showing a selection of Parisian monuments and landmarks. Make sure each slide includes the name of the monument/landmark in both English and French.
- Introduce the pictures using French, commencing each name with *Voici...* Encourage pupils to repeat the names in French. Although they are not explicitly learning these names, this nonetheless provides an excellent opportunity to engage with spoken French, and to practise pronunciation.
- Ensure that pupils are confident using the words *voici* and *c'est*; these can be used frequently in your French lessons, particularly in paired, small-group or whole-group speaking activities.
- Mini plenary: ask pupils what monument/landmark they particularly like the look of, and why.

- Monitors distribute the worksheet and reference sheet. Explain the labelling activity. Remember to prompt for a name and date on the worksheet, as you can use this to assess and monitor progress, and to offer some written feedback. If your pupils have a workbook, these should be distributed along with glue sticks. Pupils can stick the sheets into their workbooks.
- Discuss with pupils what they consider to be famous landmarks and monuments in their home country. This is particularly relevant in classes where pupils come from a number of different countries.

Plenary
5 minutes
- Remind pupils of the objectives/outcomes and ask whether they have achieved these.
- Ask learning plenary questions and note responses to inform future planning.
- Ask particularly about writing in French, for example: did they enjoy it? Does writing down the French words help them to remember what they mean in English?
- Monitors collect in workbooks/worksheets/reference sheets.

Suggestions for Parisian landmarks/monuments
- *La Tour Eiffel* The Eiffel Tower www.toureiffel.paris/fr.html
- *L'Arc de Triomphe* the Triumph Arch (in English, we call it the Arc de Triomphe) http://arc-de-triomphe.monuments-nationaux.fr/
- *Le Musée du Louvre* The Louvre (the Louvre Museum) www.louvre.fr/
- *Les Champs Élysées* The Elysian Fields (we call it the Champs-Élysées) www.champselysees-paris.com/
- *La Seine* The River Seine https://fr.wikipedia.org/wiki/Seine_à_Paris
- *Le Sacré Coeur* The Sacred Heart (the famous church situated in Montmartre; its full name in French is *La Basilique du Sacré Coeur*, and in English we call it the Sacré Coeur) www.sacre-coeur-montmartre.com/
- *La Cathédrale Notre Dame de Paris* The Cathedral of Our Lady of Paris (we call it Notre Dame) www.notredamedeparis.fr/
- *La Place de la Concorde* Harmony Square (we call it the Place de la Concorde) https://fr.wikipedia.org/wiki/Place_de_la_Concorde
- *Le Jardin des Tuileries* The Tuileries Garden www.parisinfo.com/musee-monument-paris/71304/Jardin-des-Tuileries
- *Disneyland Paris* www.disneylandparis.fr/

Lesson 3 *Ici on parle français* We speak French here

Objectives and outcomes
Today we will:
- Discover where French is spoken throughout the world
- Learn the names in French of six countries where French is spoken, and their capital cities.

French to be learned by pupils
la Belgique – Bruxelles
la Suisse – Berne
le Luxembourg – Luxembourg
le Canada – Ottawa
le Sénégal – Dakar
le Cameroun – Yaoundé

These are suggestions of six countries where French is spoken, together with their capital cities; you can also choose any from the list at the end of the lesson plan. The list features only countries where French is named as the 'official' language, so it does not include Morocco or Andorra, for example, where, although it is widely spoken, French is named as a 'recognised' language rather than an 'official' language. You can find the French names with audio files for pronunciation practice, and other interesting information, here:
www.bbc.co.uk/schools/primarylanguages/french/culture_and_places/french_speaking_world/

Resources you will need
- Map of the French-speaking countries; there are many excellent examples online.
- PowerPoint presentation or similar, with the bilingual title '*Ici on parle français!* We speak French here!', with each country where French is spoken featuring on a different slide. Given the volume of geographical information that is addressed in this lesson, it is advisable to present this in English as well as French. The focus is on understanding where French is spoken, rather than learning the names in French of all the relevant countries. The introductory slides should include the following 'language facts':
  - More than 220 million people across the world speak French!
  - English and French have a lot of very similar words, which we call 'cognates'. Can you work out what these words mean? *la France, Paris, la capitale, Londres* (they have already been introduced to these); *l'Italie, l'Afrique, l'Amérique, le Portugal, l'éléphant, les maths, la possibilité, Bon week-end! l'addition, la multiplication, le restaurant, le café, le hockey.*
- Your laminated English and French flags or other symbols to show which language you are going to be speaking.
- Sets of six 'country' cards and six 'capital' cards, with the names written in French (one set per learning pair).
- A wordsearch featuring a selection of countries, capitals and landmarks.

Getting started
5 minutes
- Hold up the laminated flag/symbol for English, to show that you will be using English.
- Introduce objectives and outcomes, including learning plenary questions, for example:
  - Name as many countries as you can where French is spoken in 30 seconds.
  - Explain what a cognate is.
  - Suggest three cognates that we looked at today.

- Now show your French flag/symbol, and to the tune of *Frère Jacques* sing the following: *la France* x 4, *l'Angleterre* x 2, *Paris et Londres* x 2, *Bon voyage!* x 2.
- Whole-group discussion about Paris, eliciting what pupils remember; ask them to articulate what they find interesting about Paris, and why.

Class activities
20 minutes
- Divide the class into two teams and nominate a pupil to be scribe. In English, ask each team to say a capital city. The team gets a point for naming the city, and the second team gets a point for saying which country it is the capital of. The scribe notes the names of each country and its capital on sheets of paper. Keep these for future lessons.
- Screen the map showing where French is spoken across the world; engage pupils in conversation about continents, as well as countries, and talk about how widespread French usage actually is.
- Screen the presentation *Ici on parle français!*, showing the names of the countries where French is the official language.
- Using the six countries and their capitals you have chosen, introduce these in French, with pupils repeating several times – for example, *Voici la Suisse. La capitale est Berne.*
- Monitors distribute the six country and six capital cards. Demonstrating that pupils should hold up the correct card, and using the instruction *Montrez-moi!* ('Show me'), call out the countries and capitals in random order in French. Pupils show that they understand what they are hearing by holding up the correct card.
- Increase the challenge by calling out the countries and capitals in English.
- Now ask in French: *Quelle est la capitale de la Belgique, de la Suisse, du Luxembourg, du Canada, du Sénégal, du Cameroun?*, again in random order. Pupils show their understanding and recall by holding up the correct card. Use a range of questioning techniques; for example, hold up a card with *Bruxelles* written on it, prompting children to hold up the relevant country card.
- Monitors distribute your wordsearch sheets for pupils to complete. These should be glued into their workbooks, or filed in their French folders.

Plenary
5 minutes
- Remind pupils of the objectives/outcomes and ask whether they have achieved these.
- Ask learning plenary questions and note responses to inform future planning.
- Ask particularly about reading in French, for example: did they enjoy finding the correct French words in the wordsearch?

Les pays francophones
French is the official language in the following countries:

Africa
Benin
Burkino Faso
Burundi
Cameroon
Central African Republic
Chad
Comoros
Democratic Republic of the Congo
Djibouti
Equatorial Guinea

Gabon
Guinea
Ivory Coast
Madagascar
Mali
Niger
Republic of Congo
Rwanda
Senegal
Seychelles
Togo

Europe
Belgium
France
Luxembourg
Monaco
Switzerland

North America
Canada
Haiti

Oceania
Vanuatu

Cross-curricular links

Art and design:
- For an enhanced focus on art, explore *Le Musée du Louvre* online at www.louvre.fr/, selecting works of art that are relevant to work you are currently doing in your art lessons.
- Recreate pictures of famous French or francophone artists such as Renoir.
- Visit www.papertoys.com/eiffel.htm.

Geography: Choose a country where French is spoken, and develop a series of exploration and discovery lessons around it. Plot a journey from your hometown to Paris by a range of different transport types.

Further learning opportunities

- Pupils can explore either their hometown or their nearest major city alongside a francophone city of their choice, and compare them.
- For a longer-term project, they can create a 'Fact File' folder that maps their own independent exploration of France and *la Francophonie*. As pupils become more familiar with France and *la Francophonie*, they can select a 'French' name for their table or learning group, for example a landmark, a country or *le Tricolore*.
- Pupils can update their bilingual vocabulary books, with the support of language list sheets.
- You will find this site useful for additional information to complement your lessons: www.timeforkids.com/destination/france.

3 Ça va? How are you?

What does the curriculum say?

Pupils should be taught to:
- *Engage in conversations; ask and answer questions; express opinions and respond to those of others.*
- *Understand basic grammar appropriate to the language being studied, including feminine and masculine forms.*

What do I need to know?

These three lessons teach basic greetings and how to introduce your family. Greetings in French can be reinforced whenever you take the class register.

The lessons use a puppet to introduce the new language. Puppets or soft toys are an excellent means of motivating children to speak in a foreign language. Pupils are often less embarrassed about making mistakes if they pretend to be someone else, and are more motivated to speak out.

Songs and rhymes are very helpful in reinforcing language and meanings, and helping pupils to memorise vocabulary. They can usefully be combined with actions; this kinaesthetic element also facilitates memorisation.

Pupils are normally intrigued by seeing photos of your own family, but if you are uncomfortable doing this there are a number of fictional or famous families to choose from, such as the Simpsons and the royal family. You may also consider it more sensitive to ask pupils to talk about fictional families.

If you would like to hear the pronunciation of this chapter's vocabulary modelled, visit www.lightbulblanguages.co.uk/resources-primary.htm where you can download podcasts, including the 'Two Little Dickie Birds' rhyme.

Comparing English with French

- *Comment ça va?* translates literally as 'How goes it?' and can be shortened to *Ça va?* An alternative way of asking someone you know how they are is *Comment vas-tu?* ('How go you?'), to which the response would be *Je vais bien.*
- Lesson 1 in this chapter introduces the grave accent (è) and the cedilla (ç). Explain to pupils that French has some additional marks to English and that these marks change the sound slightly. The grave accent makes the sound into an e sound, as in 'egg'. (The acute accent, which faces the opposite direction – é – makes the sound into an 'ay' sound, as in 'hey'.) The cedilla – ç – softens the c so that it sounds like 's'.

- *S'appeler* (to be called) is a reflexive verb, hence the additional 'reflexive pronoun': *je m'appelle, tu t'appelles.* The best English translation of the reflexive pronoun would be 'myself' or 'yourself', i.e. 'I call myself', 'you call yourself' etc.
- Lesson 3 uses the possessive pronoun 'my', which introduces the notion of gender in French. All nouns in French are one of two genders, unlike in English. There are two genders in French: masculine and feminine. The word for 'the' (definite article) with masculine nouns is *le* and the word for 'a/an' (indefinite article) is *un*. The word for 'the' with feminine nouns is *la* and the word for 'a' with feminine nouns is *une*. Possessive adjectives (my, your, his, her etc.) also reflect the gender of the nouns, so *mon* (my) is used with masculine nouns and *ma* with feminine nouns.

The French you need to teach these lessons

- *Bonjour et Au revoir* Hello and Goodbye
- The question form *Comment ça va?* and four responses (see Lesson 1)
- *Répétez* Repeat after me
- The verb *s'appeler* (to be called) in the first person (*je m'appelle*), second person (*tu t'appelles*) and third person (*il/elle s'appelle*)
- The question form of *s'appeler* in the third person: *Comment s'appelle-t-il/elle?*
- The question form *Comment ça va?* or simply *Ça va?*
- Secure pronunciation of the 'Two Little Dickie Birds' song (see Lesson 2)
- *Voici...* Here is/here are...
- Six nouns for direct family (see Lesson 3)
- The possessive adjective for 'my' in the masculine and feminine form: *mon/ma*

Lesson 1 *Enchanté* Nice to meet you

Objectives and outcomes
Today we will:
- Learn how to say hello and goodbye in French.
- Say how we're feeling and ask others how they are.

French to be learned by pupils
Bonjour Hello
Au revoir Goodbye
Comment ça va?/Ça va? How are you?
Très bien Very well
Bien Well
Comme ci, comme ça Not bad/so-so
Mal Awful
Merci Thank you

Resources you will need

- Puppet/teddy bear or other cuddly toy
- Responses to the question *Comment ça va?* displayed on the board, illustrated with relevant smiley/very smiley/so-so/sad faces

Getting started

5 minutes

- Explain that the traditional greeting in France is to kiss your friends on both cheeks. In some parts of France people kiss each other three or four times!
- Mime a kissing greeting while saying *bon-jour*, with *bon* on one cheek and *jour* on the other (*bon* = good, *jour* = day). Ask the class to repeat after you several times.
- Instruct pupils to stand up and greet and say *Bonjour* to the children around them.

Class activities

20 minutes

- Introduce a finger puppet, teddy bear or other cuddly toy to the class with *Bonjour*.
- Ask the puppet *Comment ça va?*, to which it responds *Ça va bien, merci*.
- Ask the class what the puppet was being asked, and what the response means.
- Ask several pupils *Comment ça va?* and encourage the whole class to repeat – *Répétez* – repeating one word at a time.
- Introduce different responses with gestures, asking the class to repeat after you:
  Ça va bien one thumb up
  Ça va très bien two thumbs up
  Comme ci, comme ça move your hand from side to side
  Ça va mal two thumbs down
- Practise the question and answer with individuals in the class.
- Introduce *Au revoir* on the board and with choral repetition, waving from side to side:
  Au – revoir. Repeat this with the class, saying it quietly, loudly, slowly and quickly.
- Instruct pupils to write up all new phrases from the board, illustrating the feelings by drawing smiley/very smiley/so-so/sad faces.

Plenary

5 minutes

- Model a simple dialogue with one pupil, greeting them, asking how they are, then saying goodbye.
- Pupils circulate the room, repeating the dialogue with classmates. Inform the class that the puppet will be monitoring whether any English is being used!

Lesson 2 *Comment t'appelles tu?* What are you called?

Objectives and outcomes

Today we will:

- Say what we're called.
- Ask others their names.

French to be learned by pupils

Je m'appelle... I am called...
Comment t'appelles-tu? What are you called?

Resources you will need

- Puppet or soft toy used in Lesson 1.
- The question form *Comment t'appelles-tu?* and the answer *Je m'appelle*, on display.
- The French lyrics to the song 'Two Little Dickie Birds' on display (see below).

Getting started

5 minutes

- Puppet introduces itself: *Je m'appelle Trixie.*
- Trixie says *Bonjour* to one pupil, and asks *Comment ça va?* The pupil responds, then chooses another pupil in the room to greet and ask the same question. This continues until everyone in the room has repeated the greeting and question/answer. The last person is prompted to ask Trixie.

Class activities

15 minutes

- Ask Trixie *Comment t'appelles-tu?* and display the question and answer on the board.
- Ask pupils for the meaning and remind them that they have come across the word *comment* (roughly translated as 'how') in the question *Comment ça va?*. Explain that the French translates directly as 'How are called you?'
- Trixie asks individual pupils *Comment t'appelles-tu?*
- Repeat the question with the whole class, word by word, and then the answer. Ask pupils which word means 'I' and which word means 'you' in French.
- Instruct pupils to choose the name of a famous person, without revealing it to anyone else. Pupils write the question and their fictitious name in their books.
- Explain that they're going to carry out a survey in the class. Pupils circulate the class finding out their classmates' famous identities. Trixie will be watching to make sure no one speaks any English!

Plenary

10 minutes

- Display the words to the 'Two Little Dickie Birds' song in French. Instruct the class to repeat the lines after you, performing the actions. When they are confident, try to repeat without the aid of the words.
  Deux petits oiseaux Two little birds (flap wings)
  Assis sur une branche Sitting on a branch (arm horizontal like a branch)
  Je m'appelle Fifi (finger of right hand pointing up)
  Je m'appelle Blanche (finger of left hand pointing up)
  Bonjour Fifi (nod right finger)
  Bonjour Blanche (nod left finger)
  Au revoir Fifi (right finger flies behind back)
  Au revoir Blanche (left finger flies behind back)

mon père   ma mère
le père   la mère

Lesson 3 *Ma famille* My family

Objectives and outcomes

Today we will:

- Learn how to introduce our family in French.

French to be learned by pupils

Il s'appelle He is called
Elle s'appelle She is called
Voici Here is/here are
La mère mother
La grand-mère grandmother
La soeur sister
Le père father
Le grand-père grandfather
Le frère brother
Mon my (for masculine nouns)
Ma my (for feminine nouns)

Resources you will need

- Photos of your own family/PowerPoint slides of a fictitious family/cuddly toys or puppet family members
- Worksheet with family tree template, headed *La Famille Barton/McLachlan/Smith* etc.

Getting started

5 minutes

- Ask pupils to think back to the previous lesson when they each adopted a celebrity's name. Ask the class to recall the celebrity identity of a number of their fellow pupils, and ask *Comment s'appelle-t-il/elle?* to revise the third person form of the verb.

Class activities

20 minutes

- Instruct pupils: *Écoutez* (Listen). Show them photos of your own family, or a fictional or famous family. (If you are introducing a family that is not your own, remember to introduce yourself first with *Je m'appelle …*). You can access a PowerPoint presentation with pictures of the Simpsons at www.lightbulblanguages.co.uk/resources-pr-fr-resources.htm#fam. Alternatively, you could introduce Trixie the puppet's family if you have enough puppets or cuddly toys of various sizes and genders. Introduce the photos/puppets, females first, with *Voici ma mère, Voici ma grandmère* etc.
- Show the photos/puppets again and ask pupils to translate into English.
- Ask pupils how you say 'my' in French, and why there is a difference between the word used for 'my' with feminine nouns and that used with masculine nouns. Explain that there are two genders in French, and that all nouns are either masculine or feminine.
- On the third showing, add names: *Voici ma mère. Elle s'appelle…*
- On the fourth showing, ask *Comment s'appelle-t-elle?* and ask pupils to recall the names, prompting the answer *Elle s'appelle…*

- Form pupils into 'family' groups of four and ask each to pretend to be the mother, father, brother or sister. Ask them to introduce themselves to the class.
- Sing a song to the tune of 'Westminster Chimes', which some pupils will know as 'Brownie Bells'. Sing as a class, but vary the names used in the second verse (ask pupils to volunteer the names of their mother, father, sister and brother, then take each family in turn).

    Voici ma mère
    Voici mon père
    Voici ma sœur
    Voici mon frère

    Elle s'appelle...
    Il s'appelle...
    Elle s'appelle...
    Il s'appelle...

- Pupils write up the new vocabulary on a family tree template, headed *La Famille XXX* (pupil's surname).

Plenary
5 minutes
- Ask individual pupils *Comment s'appelle ton père/ta mère?* etc. to elicit the response *Il/elle s'appelle...*

Cross-curricular links

Music: Pupils play instruments to accompany the songs or compose a tune to accompany the 'Two Little Dickie Birds' song.

Design and technology: Create a 'French-speaking' puppet, soft toy or pom-pom toy.

Registration: Reinforce the greeting and *Comment ça va?* when you take the register. You can also 'sing' the register with the following song, which uses the 'Nice One, Cyril' Tottenham Hotspur tune. It can be found on YouTube if you're not sure of the music!

Teacher sings:
Bonjour, Lottie (substitute name of child)
Comment ça va?

Pupil sings:
Très bien/Ça va bien/mal/comme ci, comme ça
Merci beaucoup

Literacy: In order to reinforce what a noun is, read a text aloud in English and instruct pupils to stand up when they hear a noun. They should sit down again when they hear another noun, e.g. 'I have a brother called John. He is 19 and lives in a flat. He has a dog called Pip and a cat called Suki.'

Further learning opportunities

- You might like to give the pupils in your class a French name. This can enhance pronunciation skills and make them aware of how some names, despite being spelt the same in English and French, are pronounced differently. Older pupils could research names and choose one for themselves. Here are some suggestions:

Girls' names	Boys' names
Amélie	Thomas
Chloé	Zacharie
Laurentine	Jean-Paul
Anouk	Xavier
Brigitte	Yves
Catherine	Serge
Aurélie	Pierre
Françoise	Matthieu
Hélène	Olivier
Sophie	Nicolas
Stéphanie	Michel
Véronique	Jacques
Simone	Henri
Monique	Jules
Chantal	David

- Pupils create and/or complete a family tree poster for inclusion in a classroom display. This should illustrate the French family member nouns by using photos or pictures of their own family or a fictitious family of their choosing. For a craft activity, they could use real leaves on their family tree!
- Introduce the question *As-tu des frères ou des soeurs?* ('Do you have any brothers or sisters?') and the responses:
  J'ai un frère/deux frères I have one/two brothers
  J'ai une soeur/deux soeurs I have one/two sisters
  J'ai une demi-soeur I have a stepsister
  J'ai un demi-frère I have a stepbrother
  Je n'ai ni frères ni soeurs I don't have any brothers or sisters
  Je suis enfant unique I am an only child

4 *Un, deux, trois...*
One, two, three...

What does the curriculum say?

Pupils should be taught to:
- *Listen attentively to spoken language and show understanding by joining in and responding.*
- *Explore the patterns and sounds of language through songs and rhymes and link the spelling, sound and meaning of words.*
- *Speak in sentences, using familiar vocabulary, phrases and basic language structures.*
- *Develop accurate pronunciation and intonation so that others understand when they are reading aloud or using familiar words and phrases.*

What do I need to know?

Lesson 1 introduces numbers 1–20. Numbers 1–10 are introduced with actions to aid memorisation. Numbers 11–20 are easier to remember as they follow similar patterns and are linked to the numbers below ten.

Lesson 2 teaches pupils how to say their age and then extends knowledge of numbers to 31, in preparation for teaching the topic of dates in the following lesson.

Lesson 3 introduces months of the year to enable pupils to say when their birthday is. The months are very similar in written form to the English but the differences in pronunciation should be highlighted. For an audio model of how to pronounce dates, visit the following website: www.bbc.co.uk/schools/primarylanguages/french/my_calendar/dates/

The following website focuses exclusively on the written form and pronunciation of French numbers: www.frenchnumbers.org.uk/

There are multiple, fun ways of reinforcing number knowledge in French as well as enhancing numeracy, including:

- Miming activities. One child makes their body into the shape of a number between one and nine, and their partner must guess the number. Numbers 10–20 can be made if pupils are in groups of three, with two making the numbers and one guessing.
- Pupils working in pairs. One child turns their back to the other child, who traces a number on his/her back. The objective is for the partner to guess the number and say it in French.
- Practise times tables and division by playing the 'fizz/buzz' game. Substitute French words for 'fizz' and 'buzz', such as *Bonjour* and *Au revoir*. Select a times table, for instance, the three times table. Taking

it in turn, pupils begin counting aloud in French from one. Every time there is a number divisible by three, the child must say *Bonjour!* To extend this and make it more challenging, run the game with two numbers, e.g. three and seven. For all numbers divisible by seven, the pupils must say *Au revoir*. You can make this more fun by asking the children to suggest their favourite French words to use; *bof* (dunno) is usually popular!

- Think of a number: *Je pense à...* Pupils take turns to guess a number (in French); you respond with either *Oui* or *Non*, then *Moins* (less) or *Plus* (more). The child who guesses the number then takes on the role of choosing a new one.

Comparing English with French

- The numbers *onze, douze, treize, quatorze* (11, 12, 13, 14) and *seize* (16) are quite easy to recall as they all have the same ending and the beginning of each resembles its <10 partner, i.e. *deux, douze; trois, treize*. *Quinze* (15) and *vingt* (20) are usually the most difficult for pupils to recall. *Dix-sept, dix-huit* and *dix-neuf* (17, 18 and 19) all follow the same pattern – ten-seven etc. – and this is worth explaining to pupils.
- Numbers above 20 are easy to form by simply adding a hyphen, e.g. *vingt-deux, vingt-cinq*. The exception is the number one, which takes *et* instead of a hyphen, i.e. *vingt et un*.
- French uses the verb 'to have' (*avoir*) to express age, rather than 'to be', as we do in English. 'I am six years old' therefore translates as 'I have six years': *J'ai six ans*.
- The 's' on the end of the word *ans* is silent and *an* is pronounced as a nasal 'on'.
- The word *âge* introduces the circumflex – sometimes presented as a little hat – which is found over some vowels. It simply shows that the vowel is a long sound.
- The months in French are written with lower-case letters, in contrast to English.

The French you need to teach these lessons

- Numbers 1–31
- *Quel chiffre est avant dix-huit?/Avant dix-huit?* Which number comes before 18?/Before 18?
- *Quel chiffre est après onze/Après onze?* Which number comes after 11?/After 11?
- The question form *Quel âge as-tu?* How old are you?, and the response *J'ai... ans.* I am... years old.
- *Combien de personnes ont 9/10 ans?* How many people are 9/10?
- The months of the year
- The question form *Quelle est la date de ton anniversaire?* When is your birthday?, and the response to the question: *C'est le...* It's the...
- *Les filles* girls *les garçons* boys
- *Le mois avant, c'est... ?* The month before is... ?
- *Le mois après, c'est... ?* The month after is... ?

Lesson 1 *Les chiffres un à vingt* Numbers 1–20

Objectives and outcomes
Today we will:
* Learn how to say the numbers 1–20 in French.

French to be learned by pupils

un 1
deux 2
trois 3
quatre 4
cinq 5
six 6
sept 7
huit 8
neuf 9
dix 10
onze 11
douze 12
treize 13
quatorze 14
quinze 15
seize 16
dix-sept 17
dix-huit 18
dix-neuf 19
vingt 20

Resources you will need
* The French words for numbers 1–20 displayed either on flashcards or on the board
* A worksheet listing the words to which pupils add digits (optional)

Getting started
2 minutes
* Ask pupils whether they already know, or can remember, any French numbers. (If you have previously covered brothers and sisters as part of the 'family' topic, low numbers will have featured.)

Class activities
25 minutes
* Introduce the numbers 1–10 with choral repetition and actions. You might like the class to help you decide on a suitable accompanying action that they will find memorable, but here are some suggestions. Some simply use gestures to help pupils memorise, while others emphasise the sound as well:

un – One hand raised
deux – Two hands raised
trois – Goldfish mouth to emphasise the *ois* sound

quatre – Catch a ball with two hands in mid-air

cinq – Hold your nose and mime 'sank'

six – Two hands sweep over each other to mime 'cease'

sept – Freeze, like a set jelly

huit – Said at speed. Hand sweeps from one side to the other, like a racing car travelling quickly at speed

neuf – Shake both hands either side of your head in an exasperated fashion to express 'getting on my nerves'

dix – Two hands elevated and wiggle fingers

- When you have repeated the numbers and actions several times together, say the first number and ask the class to say the next, then repeat backwards, from ten to one.
- Say only the number and ask the class to act out the number according to the actions decided on. Then reverse: you mime the action and the class says the number.
- Sing the numbers to the tune of '*Frère Jacques*', with one half of the class echoing the other's line:

Un, deux, trois,
Un, deux, trois
Quatre, cinq, six,
Quatre, cinq, six
Sept, huit, neuf,
Sept, huit, neuf
Dix, dix, dix,
Dix, dix, dix.

- Introduce numbers 11–20 through choral repetition. Display the numbers on card or on the board.
- Reinforce numbers 11–20 with the following games:
  - You give pupils the beginning of a number, and they complete it, e.g. *tre*…; *qu*…
  - You ask for the number that precedes or follows a number: *Quel chiffre est avant* (before) *dix-huit? Quel chiffre est après* (after) *onze?*
- Give pupils time to add the digits to a worksheet listing the words, or let pupils copy down the words from the board.

Plenary

3 minutes

- Pupils count around the room from 1 to 20. Start one chain at the front of the room and one at the back. Challenge pupils to complete the counting chains as quickly as possible; if any mistakes are made, though, the chain resumes from the beginning.

Lesson 2 *Quel âge as-tu?* How old are you?

Objectives and outcomes
Today we will:
- Learn how to say how old we are and ask others how old they are.

French to be learned by pupils
J'ai... ans I am... years old
Quel âge as-tu? How old are you?

Numbers 1–31
vingt et un 21
vingt-deux 22
vingt-trois 23
vingt-quatre 24
vingt-cinq 25
vingt-six 26
vingt-sept 27
vingt-huit 28
vingt-neuf 29
trente 30
trente et un 31
(*et* and)

Resources you will need
- Puppet or soft toy
- The question *Quel âge as-tu?* and the answer *J'ai six ans* displayed on the board
- Numbers and words 21–31 displayed either on the board or on a worksheet

Getting started
5 minutes
- Warm up by revising numbers. Say a number between one and ten and pupils hold up the correct number of fingers. Begin counting alternate numbers up to 20, with pupils filling in the gaps, then allow pupils to begin again at number one. (Teacher: *un*; class: *deux* etc.)

Class activities
20 minutes
- Let the pupils use the puppet to introduce themselves, revising greetings and *Comment ça va?*. The puppet tells the class their age, e.g. *J'ai six ans.* Ask the class for the meaning: *En anglais?*
- Choral repetition, displaying the sentence on the board. First repeat individual words, *J'ai – six – ans*, then repeat as a whole sentence. Vary choral repetition by saying 'loudly', 'quietly', 'slowly' and 'quickly'.
- Explain that French speakers say 'I *have* six years' and that we do not pronounce the 's' on the end of the word *ans*.
- The puppet asks individual pupils how old they are: *Quel âge as-tu?*
- Choral repetition of the question, shown on the board.

- Explain to the pupils that they are going to find out how many of them are one age, and how many another. If this is a Year 6 class, then children are likely to be ten or eleven; in Year 5, nine or ten. Pupils circulate the class, asking and answering the question and keeping a tally. It may help pupils to have the question and answer written down in their books, which they can refer to if needed. Model the question and answer first with one pupil.
- Ask the class *Combien de personnes ont 9/10 ans?* (How many people are 9/10?), eliciting answers in French.
- If you have a class with more than 20 pupils in it, this is the springboard for introducing numbers greater than 20.
- Show pupils the written words for numbers 21–31, asking how they are formed. They should pick out the *et* in *vingt et un* and *trente et un*; explain that this means 'and'.
- Practise reading through the numbers either with the aid of a worksheet showing digits and French words or on the board. When pupils feel more confident, they can count as a class without consulting the sheet or the board.

Plenary

10 minutes

- *Loto* game (bingo). Pupils write down five numbers in French between one and 31. If you are short of time, they can write down three. You call out the numbers in French and they circle them. The first child to have circled all of their numbers shouts *Loto!* and reads back the numbers for you to verify them.
- An alternative to the traditional game of *Loto* is to ask pupils to write five numbers horizontally. When you shout out a number on the extreme left or right of their sheet they can tear this off, remembering to keep hold of it so that they can read it out if they are the first to get a full house. Have the waste-paper basket at the ready!

Lesson 3 *Bon Anniversaire/ Joyeux Anniversaire!*
Happy Birthday!

Objectives and outcomes
Today we will:
• Learn how to say when our birthdays are.

French to be learned by pupils

les mois months
janvier January
février February
mars March
avril April
mai May
juin June
juillet July
août (pronounced 'oot') August
septembre September
octobre October
novembre November
décembre December

Quelle est la date de ton anniversaire? When is your birthday?
C'est le … It's the …
le premier the first
moins less
plus more

Resources you will need
• A set of number dominoes (example shown below), one per child
• Puppet or soft toy
• Months of the year displayed on the board
• Access to YouTube

Getting started
5 minutes
• Revise numbers 1–31. Hand out a set of dominoes; you may already have a set that you use to teach numeracy. On the left-hand side there is a sum, and on the right an answer, as shown below:

$$1 + 4 \mid 3$$

The first child reads out the sum on the left and is answered by the child who has the correct answer on their domino. This child then reads out their answer and this continues until the domino chain comes back to the first child. NB: when making the dominoes, be sure to plan them in sequence or the cycle will not be completed.

Class activities

20 minutes

- Ask the puppet when their birthday is, *Quelle est la date de ton anniversaire?*, and ask pupils to interpret what (s)he says, e.g. *C'est le vingt-quatre janvier.* (Initially avoid *août* as this is the only month that does not resemble the month in English.)
- Introduce the months of the year (*les mois*) on the board. There are a number of excellent PowerPoint presentations showing the months in French at www.tes.co.uk/teaching-resource/months-in-french-6134744.
- Choral repetition of the months, highlighting how the acute accent makes the é into an 'ay' sound. Vary the choral repetition by having girls repeat first (*les filles*), then boys (*les garçons*), then two halves of the class. Ask pupils to give you the month that precedes or follows a month, e.g. *Le mois avant* (before) *mai, c'est...?* or *Le mois après* (after) *janvier, c'est...?*
- Ask individual pupils when their birthday is and ask other pupils to interpret: *C'est le...* (It's the...) The only date that does not use the number in its usual form is 'the first', which is *le premier*.
- Pupils sing the very catchy song '*Quelle est la date de ton anniversaire?*' The soundtrack, along with slides showing the lyrics, is available at www.youtube.com/watch?v=jcwcGwaS_2w.

Plenary

5 minutes

- Pupils complete a class survey, asking when each pupil's birthday is, and complete the following table, which they draw in their jotters:

<u>Quelle est la date de ton anniversaire?</u>

NOM	ANNIVERSAIRE

Cross–curricular links

Numeracy: Give pupils simple oral addition and subtraction exercises in French, e.g. *un plus trois, c'est... ?*; *onze moins deux, c'est ... ?* Make the *Loto* game more challenging by giving pupils addition or subtraction exercises instead of simply numbers. Pupils circle the correct answer.

PE: Practise numbers in French in the playground with the following activities:

- Pupils run around in a circle until you blow the whistle. When they have stopped, call out a number in French and they must form groups containing that number of children.
- Skipping games. Pupils queue for their turn skipping over a long rope. First, state the number of people skipping together, e.g. *Deux personnes*, then the number of times they must skip, e.g. *Dix fois* (ten times). The rest of the class counts the jumps in French.

Further learning opportunities

- Pupils interview five people in French to find out their birthdays; these could include school staff or family members. They could complete the form above that they used for the class survey. Alternatively, pupils interview staff to find out who has the closest birthday to theirs.
- Introduce multiples of 10 beyond 30, up to 100:
  quarante 40
  cinquante 50
  soixante 60
  soixante-dix 70 (sixty-ten)
  quatre-vingts 80 (four twenties)
  quatre-vingt-dix 90 (four twenties and ten)
  cent 100

- Introduce days of the week so that you can habitually begin French lessons with the question *Quelle est la date aujourd'hui?* ('What's the date today?'). Pupils respond, for example *C'est lundi, le 2 octobre*. Days of the week, like months, begin with a lower-case letter:
  lundi Monday
  mardi Tuesday
  mercredi Wednesday
  jeudi Thursday
  vendredi Friday
  samedi Saturday
  dimanche Sunday

- Show pupils the short video clip (approximately three minutes' long) on the BBC Bitesize website titled 'Items for sale at a market'. This is at www.bbc.co.uk/learningzone/clips/le-vide-grenier/5699.html. Before the second viewing, ask some simple questions such as 'What do the ice skates cost?', 'If I had three euros what could I buy at the market?' or 'Which numbers do you hear in the clip?' This could be used as the basis for a simple role play.
- Play numbers noughts and crosses with the whole class in two teams, and then with pupils in pairs. The class is first divided into two teams. A noughts and crosses grid is filled with digits and pupils take it in turns to give you a number in French to indicate where they want to place their nought or cross. Pupils then prepare their own noughts and crosses grids in order to play the game in pairs.

5 *Au café* In the café

What does the curriculum say?

Pupils should be taught to:
- *Speak with increasing confidence, fluency and spontaneity, finding ways of communicating what they want to say, including through discussion and asking questions, and continually improving the accuracy of their pronunciation and intonation.*
- *Listen attentively to spoken language and show understanding by joining in and responding.*
- *Link the spelling, sound and meaning of words.*
- *Speak in sentences, using familiar vocabulary, phrases and basic language structures.*
- *Develop accurate pronunciation and intonation so that others understand when they are reading aloud or using familiar words and phrases.*

Teachers should aim to:
- *Provide opportunities for [pupils] to communicate for practical purposes.*

What do I need to know?

These lessons teach basic vocabulary for ordering snacks and drinks. French café culture plays a more important role in French life than in British life and this is worth pointing out to pupils.

The French nouns for food and drink introduced in Lesson 1 are easily accessible to English speakers and therefore easy to learn, but watch out for anglicised mispronunciation.

Lesson 2 introduces basic phrases for use in a café and revises the numbers introduced in the previous chapter to enable pupils to understand and say prices from a menu.

Lesson 3 brings together all the vocabulary learned in the first two lessons in a café role play and encourages pupils to use language with some degree of independence and creativity, using a writing template.

Comparing English with French

- Watch out for the pronunciation of *jus*: the 's' is not pronounced.
- 'Chips' in French are *des frites*. Make pupils aware that if they order *chips* in a French café or shop they will be given a bag of crisps!
- *Croque-monsieur* poses some difficulties with pronunciation, especially with the rolling of the first 'r', so will need some practice. You may want to introduce *une croque-madame* too – the same, but topped with an egg.
- *Des* is the word for 'some', used with nouns in the plural form.

- *ch* as in *chocolat chaud* is a soft sound, like 'sh'.
- *Je voudrais* ('I would like') is from the verb *vouloir* (to want) and is the conditional form of the verb.
- 'What would you like?' is *Vous désirez?*, pronounced 'dayzeeray'. Comparing this with 'You desire?' can help pupils remember it.
- 'Please' in French is *s'il vous plaît*, which translates as 'if it pleases you'.

The French you need to teach these lessons

- 10 café foods and drinks (see Lesson 1)
- How to say 'I would like', *Je voudrais*, and the corresponding question 'What would you like?', *Vous désirez?*
- The question 'How much is it?' *C'est combien?*
- The question form 'What is it?' *Qu'est-ce que c'est?*
- Phrases to construct a basic café customer-waiter dialogue
- *fort* loudly
- *doucement* quietly
- *vite* quickly
- *lentement* slowly
- *les filles* girls
- *les garçons* boys
- *C'est vrai?* Is that correct?

Lesson 1 *La nourriture et les boissons* Food and drink

Objectives and outcomes
Today we will:
- Learn the names of ten foods and drinks.

French to be learned by pupils
un jus d'orange an orange juice
un coca (light) a (diet) coke
un orangina an orangina
un chocolat chaud a hot chocolate
une eau minérale a mineral water
une limonade a lemonade
une glace an ice cream
une crêpe a pancake
un croque-monsieur a ham and cheese toastie
des frites chips
Je voudrais I would like
Vous désirez? What would you like?

Resources you will need

- A list of the new vocabulary listed above, on display
- Images representing the new words, also on display
- Flashcards or small picture cards showing the foods and drinks
- Alternatively, use props such as a plastic lemonade bottle, a coke can, a hot chocolate sachet
- The phrases *Je voudrais* and *Vous désirez?* on display

Getting started

5 minutes

- Show pupils the list of vocabulary above and ask them to work in pairs to decode the meanings of as many as possible. Draw attention to the gender of each and to *des* for the plural noun.

Class activities

20 minutes

- Work on the pronunciation of the new words through choral repetition, breaking down the longer phrases and building these up incrementally, i.e. *un, un choco, un chocolat, un chocolat chaud*. Vary the speed and volume (*lentement, vite, fort, doucement*) and switch between boys and girls (*les garçons, les filles*).
- Show a picture of a drink/snack and ask pupils to repeat after you if you say it correctly and to remain silent if you say it incorrectly. This can become a teacher vs. class competition; keep a tally of the score. Alternatively, pupils do a thumbs-up sign if you say the word correctly and thumbs down if you say it incorrectly.
- To practise those phrases that are harder to pronounce, ask pupils to cup their ears with their hands and say the phrase quietly to themselves. This creates a personal sound booth, allowing pupils to hear only their own voice.
- Lip-reading: mouth the words to the class and ask them to guess what is being said. Pupils repeat in pairs, taking it in turns to mouth the words.
- Introduce *Je voudrais* and ask pupils to guess what you're ordering. Select a food or drink, tell the class *Je voudrais un/une ...* and mime drinking or eating it. Whoever guesses it correctly is given the flashcard/picture card or object that represents the food/drink, which they then conceal.
- Show pupils the phrases *Je voudrais* and *Vous désirez?* on the board and ask for the meaning. Repeat with the whole class, and then individuals.
- Ask pupils holding the cards/objects *Vous désirez?* to elicit the response *Je voudrais ...* and the French drink/food they are holding.

Plenary

5 minutes

- Play the team game 'slap snap'. Divide the class into two teams and give each pupil a number in French. Display words or pictures of the new vocabulary for this lesson on the board. When you call out a number, the two pupils with the same number from each team come up to the front of the classroom and try to slap the corresponding picture/word as quickly as possible when you say the French word. Keep a tally of the score.

Lesson 2 *Le menu* Ordering from a menu

Objectives and outcomes

Today we will:

* Learn how to understand prices from a French menu.

French to be learned by pupils

C'est combien? How much is it?

Resources you will need

* Worksheet showing the ten new phrases and pictures introduced in the previous lesson, with phrases on one side of the sheet and pictures on the other
* Simple French café menu on display
* The French question *C'est combien?* on display
* Posters displaying café items and prices stuck on walls around the room

Getting started

5 minutes

* Pupils match up the French words learned in the previous lesson with pictures on worksheets. Whole class oral feedback.

Class activities

20 minutes

* Show pupils a simple French café menu laid out like the one below. Make the prices accessible for your class, depending on how confident they are with numbers.

	Café chocolat
Limonade	€ 3,10
Frites	€ 4,00
Chocolat chaud	€ 3,50

* Explain that euros and cents are the currency used in France and how many euros there are in one pound. Pass around some coins for pupils to handle. Plastic euro coins can also be purchased cheaply and easily on the Internet.
* Revise numbers by giving pupils a price and asking them to identify the corresponding item from the menu: *C'est quatre euros. Qu'est-ce que c'est?* Pupils respond *Des frites.*
* Play a memory game. Give pupils one minute to memorise the menu then cover up/switch off the whiteboard. (If you are using PowerPoint, clicking 'b' will obscure the slide; 'w' will reveal it again.) Repeat the previous question type and verify individuals' answers by asking the whole class *C'est vrai?*
* Introduce the question *C'est combien?* by taking on the role of the customer while the pupils are the waiters. You begin the dialogue with *Je voudrais … C'est combien?*
* Display the two phrases on the board or screen and ask pupils to practise the simple dialogue in pairs.

Plenary

10 minutes

- Running dictation. Explain that the posters on the walls show the conversation between a customer and a waiter. Pupils work in pairs, one acting as the scribe and the other as the runner. It is the job of the runner to find texts that are stuck on various walls of the classroom, memorise as much information as possible and pass this on verbally to the scribe, who must write it down as accurately as possible. The runner is not allowed to write anything down. When the pair have collected all of the lines, they must assemble them in the correct order. This activity can be made into a competition, with a prize or merit being given to the first pair that produce the most accurate text. The posters display information along the following lines:

> *Bonjour, Monsieur.*
> *Bonjour, Madame.*
> *Vous désirez?*
> *Je voudrais des frites. C'est combien?*
> *Des frites. Cinq euros.*
> *Et un coca. C'est combien?*
> *Un coca. Deux euros.*
> *Merci.*

Lesson 3 *Le café* Café role play

Objectives and outcomes
Today we will:
- Visit our own French café and order something to eat and drink.

French to be learned by pupils
s'il vous plaît please
Et pour boire? And to drink?
C'est tout? Is that everything?
Bon appétit Have a good meal

Resources you will need
- Simple café dialogue on display

Getting started
5 minutes
- Revise the question *C'est combien?* and how to say prices. Pupils note down in their jotters the price of a hot chocolate without showing anyone else. They complete a survey of the class, asking individuals *Je voudrais un chocolat chaud. C'est combien?* and jotting down the name of the person and their price. In feedback, ask pupils who has the most expensive hot chocolate, and who has the cheapest.

Class activities
20 minutes
- Present pupils with a simple café dialogue as follows:

    Bonjour, Monsieur.
    Bonjour, Madame.
    Ça va?
    Ça va très bien, merci.
    Vous désirez?
    Je voudrais un croque-monsieur, s'il vous plaît.
    Et pour boire?
    Un jus d'orange. C'est combien?
    3,20. C'est tout?
    Oui, merci.
    Bon appétit.

- Ask pupils which words are new to them (*Et pour boire?*, *C'est tout?* and *Bon appétit*) and clarify the meanings.
- Practise the dialogue with the whole class: you take on the role of the waiter and the class is the customer, then reverse.
- Pupils choose a partner and decide who is the waiter and who is the customer.
- Give pupils one minute to memorise as many of their lines as possible, then switch off the screen and ask them to read the dialogue from memory as a whole class.
- Pupils write their own dialogues, based on the model above. You can make this more authentic by rearranging the desks and chairs in the room, laying tablecloths and giving each waiter a tea towel to drape over their arm.

Plenary

5 minutes

- Pupils perform their dialogues in front of the class. While each pair perform, the rest of the class notes down which food/drink items are ordered, and how much they cost. Challenge more able pupils to perform the dialogue without referring to their lines.

Cross-curricular links

Food technology: Have a go at making a *croque-monsieur* or *crêpe* with pupils.

Registration: Pupils respond to your question *Vous désirez?* with their choice of food or drink.

Intercultural understanding: Sample French foods, e.g. *croissants*, *brie*, *crêpes* and *baguettes*.

Assembly: Pupils recreate a French café, using menus that they have produced themselves. They tell others what they have learned about French café culture and perform some café dialogues.

Further learning opportunities

- Sing along to a song contributed to the TES Resources website at www.tes.com/teaching-resource/french-song-to-taylor-swift-au-cafe-food-and-drink-6321238. It is set to 'We Are Never Ever Getting Back Together' by Taylor Swift. The lyrics are on PowerPoint and there is a YouTube link to the instrumental version.
- Pupils prepare their own French café menus, which can then be displayed or used in a 'French café' on a whole-school French day.

6 *Quelle heure est-il?*
What time is it?

What does the curriculum say?

Pupils should be taught to:
- *Listen attentively to spoken language and show understanding by joining in and responding.*
- *Engage in conversations; ask and answer questions; express opinions and respond to those of others.*
- *Speak in sentences, using familiar vocabulary, phrases and basic language structures.*
- *Develop accurate pronunciation and intonation so that others understand when they are reading aloud or using familiar words and phrases.*
- *Read carefully and show understanding of words, phrases and simple writing.*
- *Write phrases from memory, and adapt these to create new sentences, to express ideas clearly.*
- *Broaden their vocabulary and develop their ability to understand new words that are introduced into familiar written material, including through using a dictionary.*

Teachers should aim to:
- *Foster pupils' curiosity and deepen their understanding of the world.*

What do I need to know?

Learning how to tell the time in French helps to create a practical communicative context for the primary classroom. Classroom routines often include a daily timetable, showing pupils what they will be doing during the day, and at what time. Displaying a written daily schedule in French will develop pupils' familiarity with and understanding of the language, and they can take it in turns to put together each day's timetable (Chapter 8, *Quel temps fait-il aujourd'hui?*, also suggests a range of practical ideas for establishing daily routines in French). This chapter focuses on the o'clock times, to ensure that pupils feel confident with these before they are introduced to a range of times such as half past, quarter to and past, and so on. These can be confusing for children, as they don't necessarily get enough time to use, and therefore to learn, the range of time phrases.

Lesson 1 introduces pupils to twelve 'o'clock' time phrases, in both spoken and written French.

Lesson 2 looks at a range of school subjects, with a focus on listening and speaking in French, using the question *Aimes-tu...?* ('Do you like?') and the response *J'aime...* ('I like...').

Lesson 3 provides an opportunity for pupils to develop their reading skills in French by engaging with a written text addressing the language they have learned in both Lessons 1 and 2, and language addressed in earlier lessons.

Comparing English with French

- The phrase 'o'clock' changes into the plural from two to twelve o'clock, because the number of hours is more than one; for example *il est une heure, il est deux heures, il est trois heures* and so on.
- We use the preposition *à* to say 'at' one o'clock, 'at' two o'clock etc.; this preposition can also mean 'to'.
- In French, it's normal to use the definite article when talking about school subjects, for example 'I like French' is *J'aime le français* – literally, I like *the* French.
- When you ask a question by inverting the subject and the verb, always use a hyphen in French, for example: Do you like ... ? *Aimes-tu ... ?* Do you have ... ? *As-tu ... ?*

The French you need to teach these lessons

Quelle heure est-il? What time is it?

il est ... it is ...

midi midday or noon

minuit midnight

Monsieur le Loup Mr Wolf

numbers 1–12 (see Chapter 4)

à l'école at school

les matières school subjects

l'anglais English

le français French

les maths maths

l'histoire history

la géographie/la géo geography

l'informatique IT

le dessin/l'art art

les sciences science

la musique music

l'éducation physique PE

Aimes-tu ...? Do you like ...?

J'aime I like

à at

commence/termine? begins/ends

Lesson 1 *Quelle heure est-il?* What time is it?

Objectives and outcomes
Today we will:
- Learn how to tell the time in French, from one o'clock to twelve o'clock.
- Practise our French numbers and pronunciation.

French to be learned by pupils in this lesson:
[il est] une heure [It is] one o'clock
deux heures two o'clock
trois heures three o'clock
quatre heures four o'clock
cinq heures five o'clock
six heures six o'clock
sept heures seven o'clock
huit heures eight o'clock
neuf heures nine o'clock
dix heures ten o'clock
onze heures eleven o'clock
douze heures twelve o'clock

Even though the question *Quelle heure est-il?* is not part of the key language to be learned by pupils in this lesson, ensure they have the opportunity to ask the question as this will help them embed it into their longer-term vocabulary.

Resources you will need
- PowerPoint presentation or similar with the title *Quelle heure est-il?*, with individual clock faces showing one o'clock to twelve o'clock
- Differentiated bingo cards, with a range of clock faces, and times written in French/English. If you can, laminate your bingo cards, and ensure pupils use erasable pens, as you will get repeated use from the same cards (see **Bloomsbury Online Resource 6A**)

Getting started
5 minutes
- Indicate that you will be using English as a means of communication, and explain the objectives for today's lesson.
- At high speed, practise the o'clock times in English; this can be a blend of 'drilling' and discussion; for example, 'What time do we normally have our maths lesson?' 'What time do we normally have our morning break?' and so on.
- In French, recite the numbers 1–12, indicating that pupils should join in; do this several times, increasing speed each time.
- For increased challenge, recite the numbers backwards.
- For additional support, use the melody of 'Frère Jacques' to practise the numbers; this works very well for the 'o-clock' times: *un, deux, trois* (x2); *quatre, cinq, six* (x2); *sept, huit, neuf* (x2), *dix, onze, douze* (x2).

Class activities
20 minutes
- Screen the presentation *Quelle heure est-il?* Pointing to a clock face, ask pupils to predict what the question might mean *en anglais*.

- Work through the 12 clock times, with *Quelle heure est-il?* as the title banner on each slide to reinforce the question; show the clock face first, saying *Il est une heure, Il est deux heures* and so on, with the phrase appearing after pupils have repeated the phrase in French.
- Screen clock faces in random order, asking *Quelle heure est-il?* For additional support, offer a selection of written time phrases on the slide from which they can select.
- Screen a range of time phrases in random order in French, asking what they mean *en anglais*.
- Now screen the phrases in English, asking what they mean *en français*. This is more challenging, so they may need additional supportive prompting.
- Monitors distribute the bingo cards. Nominate the 'winning word', for example *La France, le croissant* or *la Tour Eiffel*.
- Repeat the bingo game, increasing the challenge each time. After each game, pupils wipe the crosses off their bingo card (if laminated) and swap with another pupil, to ensure they experience a range of vocabulary. Ask the winner to read out each phrase on his or her card, as this is additional reinforcement and also confirms their 'win'.

Plenary

5 minutes

- Oral 'whizz quiz': call out a random range of time phrases in French and pupils call out the corresponding phrase in English; then reverse.
- Remind pupils of the objectives/outcomes and ask whether they have achieved these.

Lesson 2 *À l'école* At school

Objectives and outcomes

Today we will:

- Learn to recognise and say 6/8/10 school subjects in French (select a number that is appropriate for your class).
- Learn how to say what subjects we like.
- Listen to people talking in French, and speak in our best French accent.

French to be learned by pupils

- A range of school subjects from the list above appropriate to your class; six works well for Years 3/4 and eight for Years 5/6 in the first instance
- *J'aime ...* I like

Resources you will need

- Internet access/audio to screen the short clip about school here: www.educationscotland.gov.uk/resources/a/animatedfrenchresource/alecole.asp
- PowerPoint presentation or similar with the title *À l'école*, including individual slides showing the name of your selected school subjects; use images to illustrate the words
- Sets of *Oui/Non* response cards (see **Bloomsbury Online Resource 6B**)

Getting started

5 minutes

- Indicate that you will be using English as a means of communication, and explain the objectives for today's lesson.
- In order, show clock faces from one to 12 o'clock, asking *Quelle heure-est il?* Repeat in random order, accepting *deux heures, trois heures* and so on as a correct answer, as well as the complete phrase, for example *il est deux heures, il est trois heures*. After each response, repeat the phrase in full, as this helps to reinforce the phrase for the whole class.
- Ask pupils what subjects they do in school, and note these on your whiteboard. Ask them which subjects they like.

Class activities

20 minutes

- Screen the presentation *Á l'école*. Using an image of a school, or an object associated with school on the title slide, ask whether they can predict what the phrase means *en anglais*.
- Begin the presentation with the short clip from Education Scotland's website www.educationscotland.gov.uk/resources/a/animatedfrenchresource/alecole.asp. A transcript is also available for reference; this is also an excellent way to refresh language addressed in Chapter 2.
- Discuss the clip with the pupils, asking them what they were able to understand, how 'French' the words sounded and so on. Where time allows, show the transcript, and ask individual pupils to read sentences out loud; alternatively, the whole group can read out loud together.
- Screen your selected school subjects; the header for each slide is *Les matières*.
- Pupils repeat each phrase, with a focus on sounding as 'French' as possible, similar to the French they heard.

- Demonstrate how to use to *Oui/Non* cards. For example, holding up the *Oui* card, say *Aimes-tu l'histoire? Oui!*, reinforcing the meaning of *Oui!* with a 'thumbs up'. Now do exactly the same with the *Non* card, using a thumbs down.
- Monitors distribute the *Oui/Non* cards. Ask a whole-group series of questions: *Aimes-tu ... ?* Pupils can respond entirely non-verbally, simply using the card, or with the appropriate word as well as the card. After the whole-group response, ask individual children. This is best done at high speed to ensure the pace does not lag.
- Now ask the same questions, demonstrating the response *Oui, j'aime l'histoire*. In this lesson, the focus is not on forming negative sentences in French, so each response will begin with *Oui*. Show that this is the response you require by holding up your own *Oui* card. Try to include as many children as possible in the elicitation of a whole-phrase oral response.

Plenary
5 minutes

- Oral 'whizz quiz' addressing both o'clock times and your selected school subjects. It is essential that children have a lot of opportunity to practise these phrases.
- Remind pupils of the objectives/outcomes and ask whether they have achieved these.

Lesson 3 *Une journée à l'école* A day at school

Objectives and outcomes

Today we will:

- Read about a French school day.
- Look at some new French words, and work out what they mean in English.
- Practise our French pronunciation by reading out loud in French.

French to be learned by pupils

This lesson is essentially a consolidation of language addressed in Lessons 1 and 2, and also in earlier chapters, such as days of the week. However, one of its key learning goals is to encourage pupils to predict the meaning of new words, using a range of strategies. These include:

commence à... begins at...
la récréation (or *la récré*) break
le déjeuner lunch
termine à... ends at...
J'arrive à l'école à... I arrive at school at...
à midi at midday
après-midi afternoon

Resources you will need

- Mini whiteboards
- *Oui/Non* cards
- PowerPoint presentation or similar, with the title
- The written text, which is outlined below
- Differentiated gap exercise (see **Bloomsbury Online Resource 6C**)

Getting started

5 minutes

- Indicate that you will be using English as a means of communication, and explain the objectives for today's lesson.
- Using mini whiteboards, call out a selection of 'o'clock' times and school subjects, starting with French, and pupils note these in English on their whiteboards. Say *Montrez-moi*, and pupils hold up their boards to show you their written response. Now do the same using the English phrase: this gives pupils an informal opportunity to practise writing in French, and also to recall their French vocabulary.
- You may like to introduce a game of 'What's the time, Mr Wolf?' (*'Quelle heure est-il, Monsieur le Loup?'*) if time allows; pupils will be familiar with this game from their English lessons.

Class activities

20 minutes

- Monitors distribute the reading text; it is also useful to screen it on your whiteboard.
- Read the text out loud, enunciating very carefully and clearly.
- Ask pupils whether there are words they know and/or recognise; encourage them to predict meanings by focusing on cognates or near cognates. The text includes words that they are not explicitly learning, for example *les leçons* and *immédiatement*, but one of the learning goals

is to encourage pupils to understand that they do not need to know every word in order to understand the overall meaning. It is also a successful strategy for 'implicitly' learning new language.

- Reading in the round: individual pupils take turns to read each sentence out loud; encourage them to use their best French accent. You can select pupils or ask for volunteers. It is useful to keep a record of which children seem either enthusiastic or reluctant to read out loud, as this can help you plan future activities to ensure that both the enthusiasm and reluctance are addressed equally.

Bonjour! Je m'appelle Mehdi. J'arrive à l'école à huit heures. Les leçons commencent immédiatement. La première leçon est les maths. La deuxième leçon commence à neuf heures. C'est l'anglais ou le français. Après la récré, c'est l'histoire ou la géo. À midi nous prenons le déjeuner. La quatrième leçon commence à une heure. Le lundi, mercredi et vendredi c'est les sciences. Le mardi c'est l'éducation physique ou l'art. Le jeudi c'est la musique. J'aime bien le français, l'histoire et les maths. L'école termine à trois heures. Au revoir!

- Discuss the meaning of the text; this can be a useful introduction to translating into English, helping children to understand that English and French don't work in exactly the same way.
- Ask a range of 'meaning' questions in which pupils have to translate your given sentences, such as '*En anglais ... Je m'appelle Mehdi, j'aime bien le français*'. For an additional challenge, ask them to translate from English to French, for example: '*En français ... The second lesson begins at nine o'clock, and school finishes at three o'clock.*'
- Distribute the gap exercise (**Bloomsbury Online Resource 6C**) for pupils to complete. You may like to make your own exercise sheet: to ensure that they are kept occupied, it is useful to provide three or four differentiated activities on a single, double-sided sheet. Give pupils the challenge of completing at least one activity within the allocated time.

Plenary
5 minutes

- Discuss reading in French with pupils: has it helped them to remember their new French words? Has it helped them to learn some new words?
- Remind pupils of the objectives/outcomes and ask whether they have achieved these.

Cross-curricular links

English (literacy and oracy): Focus on whole-group, small-group and paired discussion and learning activities, both verbal and in writing; pupils will find the following short clip interesting: www.timeforkids.com/destination/france/day-in-life. Use this as a starting point for creating 'daily timelines' in English.

Further learning opportunities

- Pupils can create their own version of the text in Lesson 3, using the original as a writing frame; these make a great learning display for the classroom.
- Explore school life around the world, comparing children's experiences in different countries. This is a good starting place: www.infoplease.com/world/statistics/school-years.html.
- Discuss particular differences in school life; there are several topics that can encourage lively debate, and help children to develop their speaking skills in English, such as the following:
  - French state schools do not require pupils to wear any kind of uniform.
  - Explore the French tradition of *la rentrée* – this literally means 'the return', and it is a major event in the annual French calendar, when French children return to school after a long summer break. Lots of grown-ups have a long summer break too, and *la rentrée* also refers to their return to work.
  - In France, parents have to buy everything that children need for learning in school, and pupils have to bring it to school with them in their special school bag, known as *le cartable*.
- The BBC Languages website has a series of useful film clips and audio files, as well as games, to practise language, which bring together language from this and other chapters. For example:
  www.bbc.co.uk/schools/primarylanguages/french/school_day/
  www.bbc.co.uk/schools/primarylanguages/french/school_day/school_subjects/

7 C'est bon pour la santé!
Being healthy!

What does the curriculum say?

Pupils should be taught to:
* *Listen attentively to spoken language and show understanding by joining in and responding.*
* *Engage in conversations; ask and answer questions; express opinions and respond to those of others.*
* *Speak in sentences, using familiar vocabulary, phrases and basic language structures.*
* *Develop accurate pronunciation and intonation so that others understand when they are reading aloud or using familiar words and phrases.*
* *Read carefully and show understanding of words, phrases and simple writing.*
* *Write phrases from memory, and adapt these to create new sentences, to express ideas clearly.*
* *Understand and respond to spoken and written language from a variety of authentic sources.*
* *Broaden their vocabulary and develop their ability to understand new words that are introduced into familiar written material, including through using a dictionary.*

Teachers should aim to:
* *Foster pupils' curiosity and deepen their understanding of the world.*

What do I need to know?

Talking about healthy foods and lifestyles is something that is very familiar to primary school pupils from their work in science and other curriculum areas. Learning the words for fruit and vegetables in French is a successful introductory way of integrating these themes into French lessons, and promoting a cross-curricular approach.

Lesson 1 introduces pupils to a selection of fruits and vegetables, in both spoken and written French.

Lesson 2 links language from Chapter 6, 'What time is it?', and looks at how to say a sentence in the negative form. It also provides pupils with an opportunity to express opinions about foods that are considered healthy or unhealthy.

Lesson 3 moves on to parts of the body, and uses a familiar song ('Head, shoulders, knees and toes') to practise these words. This provides an excellent starting point for some creative writing and dictionary work.

Additional notes

You will be covering quite a lot of new French in these three lessons. Whilst there are lots of opportunities for them to practise this new language in the individual lessons, it will still take quite a lot of additional practice time for them to be able to recall and reuse it. For the three lessons following these ones, you should therefore focus on revisiting and practising, and avoid introducing any new language.

Comparing English with French

- We tend to use the term 'fruit' to mean fruits in the plural, but it is always plural in French: *les fruits*.
- Although *fruits* is certainly a 'visual' cognate, it is not an 'aural' one – *fruits* is pronounced as *fwee*, i.e. both the r and the s are silent, and the vowel combination or sound *ui* is pronounced 'wee'.
- *La salade* means both salad and lettuce. Another word for lettuce is *la laitue*.
- The song 'Head, Shoulders, Knees and Toes' (*'Tête, épaules, genoux et pieds'*) is usually sung without definite articles in French; however, singing it with the definite article (*la tête, les épaules, les genoux, les pieds*) is also acceptable, and is a great way of practising articles and genders.
- *Les yeux* is the plural for 'eyes'. The singular form for 'eye' looks quite different: *un œil*.
- We use 'hair' in the singular in English, but in French we always use the plural form, *les cheveux*.
- The word for toe, *orteil*, becomes *l'orteil* when you use the definite article. This is because we use an apostrophe when the noun begins with a vowel. There are a few exceptions, though!
- However, the French version of the song uses the word *pieds* (feet), rather than toes.
- As in English, most plural words are formed by adding 's'; however, *le genou* (knee) requires the letter x, and becomes *les genoux*. Other high-frequency nouns that add an x are: *le cheveu, les cheveux* (hair); *le cheval, les chevaux* (horse, horses); *le drapeau, les drapeaux* (flag, flags); *le gâteau, les gâteaux* (cake, cakes); *le château, les châteaux* (castle, castles); *le hibou, les hiboux* (owl, owls).

The French you need to teach these lessons

- *les fruits et légumes* Fruit and vegetables
- *Quel mot manque?* Which word is missing?
- *Ma liste de courses* My shopping list
- *C'est bon pour la santé?* Is it/are they good for your health?
- *C'est mauvais pour la santé?* Is it/are they bad for your health?

Lesson 1 *Les fruits et légumes* Fruit and vegetables

Objectives and outcomes

Today we will:

- Learn how to say six fruits and six vegetables in French (or the number most appropriate for the age of the group).
- Say which fruits and vegetables we like.

French to be learned by pupils

les pommes apples
les oranges oranges
les pêches peaches
les poires pears
les fraises strawberries
les bananes bananas
les pommes de terre potatoes
les choux cabbages
les choux-fleurs cauliflowers
les carottes carrots
les petits pois peas
les haricots verts green beans

Resources you will need

- A3 sheets of paper, one per table, with marker pens for pupils to write with.
- PowerPoint presentation number 1, *Les fruits et les légumes*, which shows images of the fruits and vegetables you have selected, one per slide., together with the written phrase which should appear at the bottom of the slide, after a second click of the mouse
- The presentation should include slides of the pictures in random order, with the correct word appearing on a second click
- PowerPoint presentation number 2: repeat the slides but this time delete two or three of the images, so that only the text is visible
- PowerPoint presentation number 3: show each fruit and vegetable, but this time with the phrase *J'aime les pommes, J'aime les poires* and so on
- Set of laminated picture cards, with a fruit or vegetable on each card, one set per learning pair (see **Bloomsbury Online Resource 7A**)

Getting started

5 minutes

- Introduce objectives and outcomes.
- Oral recap of language addressed in the previous lesson, with questions beginning *Aimes-tu...?*, prompting pupils to respond *Oui, j'aime...*
- Using the symbol for using English, initiate a whole-group discussion about 'healthy foods'.
- In table groups, pupils jot down as many fruits and vegetables in English as they can in one minute.
- Whole-group sharing of the fruits and vegetables they came up with; select from the list those you have chosen to focus on in French. Keep the sheets for future use to facilitate learning when pupils will be working with bilingual dictionaries (see 'Further learning opportunities').

Class activities

20 minutes

- Screen PowerPoint presentation number 1, displaying each image and clicking to show the related text. Enunciate each word carefully; pupils repeat.
- Go through the slides in presentation 1 again, but this time initially show just the pictures, and ask questions that prompt pupils to identify the fruit and vegetables, e.g. *Les pommes, oui ou non? Les carottes, oui ou non?* and so on. Pupils respond with *Oui/Non*, then you click to reveal the correct word.
- Now move on presentation 2 in which the pictures of some fruit/vegetables are missing, and ask *Quel mot manque?* Demonstrate the first response, and children will understand what the question means without your explaining it in English.
- Using the instruction *Montrez-moi*, call out fruits and vegetables in random order in French; using the picture cards in **Bloomsbury Online Resource 7A**, pupils demonstrate their understanding by holding up the card with the correct fruit or vegetable.
- Move on to PowerPoint presentation 3: the slides with the phrase beginning with *J'aime…*. Pupils repeat several times.
- Practise the phrase by asking *Aimes-tu … ?*
- For additional challenge, add some 'new' words that children do not know, for example *Aimes-tu les oignons* (onions), *les tomates* (tomatoes), *le brocoli* (broccoli), *la salade* (salad or lettuce)… encourage them to try and identify these items and then respond to the question.

Plenary

5 minutes

- Pupils put the card sets into their envelopes, and monitors collect them.
- Divide the class into two teams: *fruits* and *légumes*.
- At high speed, call out in a blend of English and French any words that you have worked on today, or in the previous lesson. Where you call out in French, pupils respond in English and vice versa. *Un point* for answers *en anglais* and *deux points* for answers *en français*. This works best as a 'shout it out' game, where they can simply call out an answer; the first to respond correctly wins the point or points for their team.
- Remind pupils of the objectives/outcomes and ask whether they have achieved these (thumbs up, thumbs down).

Lesson 2 *La nourriture qui est bon pour votre santé*
Food that's good for you

Objectives and outcomes
Today we will:
- Learn how to say which fruits and vegetables we don't like.
- Think about foods that are good or bad for our health.
- Learn six fruits and six vegetables in French (or the number most appropriate for the age of the group).

French to be learned by pupils
Je n'aime pas… I don't like…
C'est bon pour la santé It's good for your health
C'est mauvais pour la santé It's bad for your health
mais (pronounced 'may') but
et (pronounced 'ay' as in 'may') and

Resources you will need
- Mini whiteboards and pens
- PowerPoint presentation or similar, *C'est bon pour la santé* : the slides should show between 8 and 12 images of fruit and vegetables; you could simply reuse the slides from Lesson 1, but add the question on each slide: *C'est bon pour la santé?*
- A second PowerPoint presentation, also between 8 and 12 slides, with images of foods you consider unhealthy, and the phrase *C'est mauvais pour la santé*
- A final presentation: between 8 and 12 slides showing *bon/mauvais* foods in a random order
- Reuse the slides in any order, with the question *Aimes-tu … ?* for the title banner and the phrase *Non, je n'aime pas … les pommes, les poires* and so on at the bottom of the slide
- Set of two picture cards, one with a tick, one with a cross

Getting started
5 minutes
- Introduce objectives and outcomes.
- Using the mini whiteboards, pupils draw a six-square bingo grid, and write in English any six fruits or vegetables, one per square. If they are unfamiliar with this routine, demonstrate it first on your own mini whiteboard, then ask a pupil to repeat the instructions in English.
- Play several games of bingo, calling out the words in French. Select a suitable winning word or phrase, for example *J'aime les fruits et les légumes!* The winner must read out all six words so that you can check that the 'win' is accurate.
- If there is time, increase the bingo challenge by asking pupils to write the words in French (but reassure them it doesn't matter if they can't remember the correct spelling!).

Class activities
20 minutes
- Screen the first PowerPoint presentation, fruit and vegetables, saying each time *C'est bon pour la santé*; pupils repeat the phrase. Use thumbs up to illustrate 'good'.
- Now screen the presentation with pictures of foods you consider 'unhealthy', saying *C'est mauvais* each time; they repeat the phrase. Use thumbs down to illustrate 'bad'.
- Show the *bon/mauvais* picture slides (presentation 3), asking whether the foods shown are *bon/mauvais pour la santé*. Keep using thumbs up, thumbs down to illustrate the meaning of *bon/mauvais*.

- Reuse the slides in any order, with the question *Aimes-tu ...?*, with the phrase *Non, je n'aime pas ... les pommes, les poires* and so on at the bottom of the slide.
- Pupils repeat the phrase several times.
- Selecting individual pupils, and holding up the picture card with either the cross or the tick, ask *Aimes-tu ...?*
- Pupils respond according to the cross/tick card, for example *Oui, j'aime les choux-fleurs* or *Non, je n'aime pas les choux*.
- For increased challenge, model several examples of more complex sentences, for example *J'aime les pommes, mais je n'aime pas les pommes de terre* or *J'aime les bananes, mais je n'aime pas les poires*, and encourage pupils to create their own sentences.

Plenary

5 minutes

- The plenary game is a whole-class memory game. Explain the rules in English. The game is called *Je vais au marché pour...* ('I'm going to the market for...'). The first person says, for example, *Je vais au marché pour les pommes*. The second person says *Je vais au marché pour les pommes et les poires*. The third person says *Je vais au marché pour les pommes, les poires et les choux*, and so on. This works well with all children standing. When a pupil cannot remember the correct order, he or she sits down. The pupil (or pupils) left standing win/s.
- Remind pupils of the objectives/outcomes and ask whether they have achieved the outcomes (thumbs up, thumbs down).

Lesson 3 *Mon corps* My body

Objectives and outcomes

Today we will:

- Learn how to say parts of the body.
- Learn and sing a new song in French.

French to be learned by pupils

- Choose an appropriate number of words from the following list, but include 'head', 'shoulders', 'knees', 'toes', 'eyes', 'ears', 'mouth' and 'nose', as you will be using these in the song.

  la bouche mouth
  le bras (les bras) arm (arms)
  la dent (les dents) tooth (teeth)
  l'épaule (les épaules) shoulder (shoulders)
  le genou (les genoux) knee (knees)
  la jambe leg
  la joue cheek
  la main hand
  le nez (les nez) nose (noses)
  l'oreille (les oreilles) ear (ears)
  l'orteil (les orteils) toe (toes)
  le pouce thumb
  la tête head
  le visage face
  les yeux eyes

Resources you will need

- PowerPoint or similar presentation featuring the parts of the body you have selected, illustrated with a suitable image
- YouTube clip of the song '*Tête, épaules, genoux et pieds*' (the French version literally translates as 'Heads, shoulders, knees and feet'): www.youtube.com/watch?v=0EFXCdryyRM
- 'Match-up' body worksheet with pictures and words (see **Bloomsbury Online Resource 7B**)

Getting started

5 minutes

- Introduce objectives and outcomes.
- Ask pupils to stand up: *Levez-vous*.
- Use the symbol for English and sing the song 'Head, Shoulders, Knees and Toes', using actions to point to the parts of the body; encourage the class to join in.
- Now sing the French version to the children:
  Tête, épaules, genoux et pieds,
  Genoux et pieds,
  Tête, épaules, genoux et pieds,
  Genoux et pieds,
  J'ai deux yeux, deux oreilles, une bouche et un nez,
  Tête, épaules, genoux et pieds – genoux et pieds!

- You may prefer to sing the version using the definite article; the wording is slightly different:

  La tête, les épaules, les genoux et les pieds x 2

  Les yeux, les oreilles, la bouche et le nez,

  La tête, les épaules, les genoux et les pieds x 1

Class activities

20 minutes

- Screen the presentation of parts of the body; pupils repeat several times.
- To practise the words, use the song in French; ask pupils to stand up (*Levez-vous*) and to sing (*Chantez*).
- Play *Jacques a dit* ('Simon says…'). Pupils remain standing up; if they are unfamiliar with the game, explain in English.
- Start each instruction with *touchez*; for example, *Jacques a dit touchez le nez, Jacques a dit touchez les épaules*. Increase speed a little and introduce instructions without *Jacques a dit*; children who still touch that particular part of the body have to sit down. Whoever remains standing wins the game. For additional challenge include a range of language from other contexts, for example *Jacques a dit asseyez-vous, Jacques a dit fermez les yeux* and *Jacques a dit ouvrez les yeux*.
- Distribute match-up worksheets for pupils to complete; glue into their workbooks or file in their French folders.

Plenary

5 minutes

- Play 'shout it out'! Randomly call out individual words in French; pupils respond with the corresponding word in English. Then call out a series of words in English; pupils respond in French. They will particularly enjoy the game if they don't know which language you are going to call out in!
- Remind pupils of the objectives/outcomes and ask whether they have achieved these (thumbs up, thumbs down).

Cross-curricular links

Science/maths:

- Using a survey template that pupils are familiar with from science or maths lessons, carry out a *sondage* (survey) to identify pupils' likes and dislikes, highlighting the most and least popular fruits and vegetables.
- Discuss the cost of fruit and vegetables, and allocate pairs of children a certain amount of money. Give them a shopping list from which they must work out what they can afford to buy.

IT:

- Explore daily menus from French primary schools, using the Internet. Although pupils will not understand every word, with the support of a bilingual dictionary, and by using strategies such as identifying cognates or near cognates, they will be able to understand the majority of the text. Use the following search terms: *menus maternelles, menus élémentaires*.
- Select a French shop online, and let pupils explore how much fruit and vegetables cost, comparing that to what they know about the price of fruit and vegetables in their home country. Try the Paris Carrefour: www.carrefour.fr/magasin/paris-auteuil.

Art/design:

- Following on from the work with menus, select a series of images online; pupils design not only the menus for the week, but also the visual aspect of their menu. This works well in pairs.

Further learning opportunities

- Pupils create shopping lists for each other. This is an excellent opportunity to include foodstuffs other than fruit and vegetables at this early stage. This has a dual focus on reading and creative writing in French.
- Exploring the French language version of 'The Very Hungry Caterpillar', *La chenille qui fait des trous* (literally 'The caterpillar who makes holes'), over a series of lessons is a great longer-term literacy project. The book is available in a variety of formats in most high street and online bookshops. SparkleBox also offers a range of artwork based on the story. The language features days of the week, some high-frequency verbs and a range of foodstuffs, which is an excellent way of both revisiting and reinforcing language already covered, as well as introducing new language. Children are very familiar with the story in English, which acts as a great springboard for further learning in French.
- Similarly, the French language version of 'Go Away, Big Green Monster!', *Va t'en, grand monstre vert!*, is a really successful resource for French, and for cross-curricular learning. Engaging with longer texts at such an early stage in their French learning can really help children to develop a love of reading – in both French and English.
- An online search will provide you with numerous examples of presentations of both stories in French. You will also see some examples with the title *La chenille affamée* (literally 'The hungry caterpillar') but it is better to use the title *La chenille qui fait des trous* in keeping with the book versions.
- There is a delightful video clip on YouTube of French primary school children reading *La chenille qui fait des trous* out loud. The video shows the book pages, so that pupils can follow the text as they hear it. If you decide to use it, check first that your school's firewalls don't prohibit the streaming of clips from YouTube. www.youtube.com/watch?v=xBpHkMgWId8
- Create a learning display of healthy foods; paper plates are a great craft resource.
- Use the song '*Savez-vous planter les choux?*' to practise other parts of the body. This also provides an excellent opportunity for creative writing: write new verses using different parts of the body, and for dictionary work, as pupils choose their own words for their new verses.
- An excellent clip of the song '*Savez-vous planter les choux?*' is available on YouTube at www.youtube.com/watch?v=iAGV2pcLaAg. The lyrics are as follows:

Savez-vous planter les choux	Do you know how to plant cabbages?
À la mode, à la mode	Like …
Savez-vous planter les choux	Do you know how to plant cabbages?
À la mode de chez nous	Like we do?
On les plante avec les pieds	We plant them with our feet
On les plante avec le genoux	We plant them with our knees
On les plante avec le nez	We plant them with our noses
On les plante avec le coude	We plant them with our elbows

- Use bilingual dictionaries suitable for primary-age children (see recommendations on page xviii of the Introduction); alternatively, computers/tablets with online access to www.wordreference.com.

8 *Quel temps fait-il aujourd'hui?* What's the weather like today?

What does the curriculum say?

Pupils should be taught to:
* *Listen attentively to spoken language and show understanding by joining in and responding.*
* *Engage in conversations; ask and answer questions; express opinions and respond to those of others.*
* *Speak in sentences, using familiar vocabulary, phrases and basic language structures.*
* *Develop accurate pronunciation and intonation so that others understand when they are reading aloud or using familiar words and phrases.*
* *Read carefully and show understanding of words, phrases and simple writing.*
* *Write phrases from memory, and adapt these to create new sentences, to express ideas clearly.*

Teachers should aim to:
* *Foster pupils' curiosity and deepen their understanding of the world.*

What do I need to know?

Learning how to talk about the weather in French is perfect for the Primary French classroom. It can be included in the daily communicative routine of both the classroom and the whole school, and provides a framework for exploring the wider world. Establish the routine of writing the day, date and weather at the beginning of the day in a prominent place in the classroom. This works particularly well with picture prompts and labels that pupils can select and stick on a display board. The weather display can change at focus points during the day, with pupils taking turns, for example after morning break and after lunchtime. This encourages pupils to use their French for very practical purposes, and to engage with French on a regular basis throughout the day.

Lesson 1 introduces pupils to eight simple weather phrases, in both spoken and written French.

Lesson 2 links language from Chapter 2 (*Bonjour La France et la Francophonie!*) and pupils children with an opportunity to explore some major French cities, with a focus on developing speaking and creative writing skills.

Lesson 3 is about primary and secondary colours, with a focus on developing reading skills in French.

Bonus French

- Add to your bank of French idioms with *Après la pluie, le beau temps*. The translation is 'After the rain comes the good weather' and the English equivalent is 'Every cloud has a silver lining'.

Comparing English with French

- The double 'll' in *brouillard* is pronounced 'y', similar to *juillet*.
- Weather phrases work slightly differently in French. We use *il y a* (there is, there are) when we have a noun, such as *vent* (wind), *soleil* (sun) and *brouillard* (fog). If we are using an adjective such as *froid* (cold) or *chaud* (hot), the verb *faire* (to do, to make) is required: *il fait froid*, *il fait chaud* and so on.
- The question *Quel temps fait-il?* can also cause some confusion: it literally means *What weather does it do?*
- We use the preposition *à* when referring to cities or towns, e.g. *Il fait beau à Paris, à Montréal, à Bruges*, but when we are referring to countries, we use a range of prepositions, for example *en France* (feminine countries), *au Canada* (masculine countries) and *aux États Unis* (countries that are expressed in the plural).

The French you need to teach these lessons

- Question formats: *Quel? Quelle?* What?; *C'est quelle ville?* Which city is it?; *C'est de quelle couleur?* What colour is it?
- 8–12 weather phrases (see Lesson 1)
- City and country names with the relevant prepositions *à/en*
- 8–12 colours (see Lesson 3)
- *le temps* weather
- *aujourd'hui* today
- *il y a* there is, there are
- *voici* here is, here are
- *un arc-en-ciel* a rainbow
- *la couleur/les couleurs* the colour/the colours
- *les couleurs primaires/secondaires* primary/secondary colours

---

Lesson 1 *Quel temps fait-il aujourd'hui?* What's the weather like today?

Objectives and outcomes

Today we will:

- Learn how to ask what the weather is like in French.
- Learn how to describe the weather in our best French accent.

French to be learned by pupils

il fait chaud it's hot

il fait beau it's lovely

il y a du soleil it's sunny

il fait froid it's cold

il pleut it's raining

il neige it's snowing

il y a du vent it's windy

il y a du brouillard it's foggy

Resources you will need

- Online map of France. There are many excellent maps and posters available online, with a range of font types and sizes and highlighted regions, rivers, mountains, landmarks and so on. Select the most appropriate for your pupils.
- PowerPoint presentation or similar resource with images of a range of weather types; include slides that show both image and phrase
- Set of small 'types of weather' picture cards for pupils (see **Bloomsbury Online Resource 8A**); one set between three or four pupils is sufficient. To increase the challenge a little, you might like to include between two and four additional weather types. If possible, laminate the cards so that you can reuse them over a number of years. Keep each set separately in small zipped, transparent folders
- Companion set of 'types of weather' word cards, with the phrases written in French (see **Bloomsbury Online Resource 8B**). For additional support, you may wish to make the cards bilingual by adding the English translation
- Optional: bilingual vocabulary books and language list sheets

Getting started

5 minutes

- Oral guessing game with language addressed in the previous lesson. Alternatively, you can select any area of language you have already worked on and revisit: frequent revisiting in random order helps pupils to embed their French.
- Introduce objectives and outcomes, including learning plenary questions, for example:
  - 30 seconds to describe what we did in French today.
  - 30 seconds to talk about what we learned in French today.
  - Tell me three things you can now say in French that you couldn't say at the beginning of the lesson.
- Whole-group questioning in English about weather types.
- Prompt pupils to think about the weather we normally expect in different seasons.
- Prompt pupils to think about weather types in different countries.

Class activities

25 minutes

- Present the eight weather types aurally using picture prompts only, each time asking *Quel temps fait-il?*
- Pupils repeat each phrase several times; ensure that pupils also have the opportunity to practise asking the question.
- Practise the phrases using a range of basic questioning techniques, for example:
  - *Oui ou non?*
  - *Vrai ou faux?*
  - *Qu'est-ce qui manque?*
- Repeat the presentation of weather types, this time including the written phrase with the appropriate picture.
- Monitors distribute the weather picture cards. Using the instruction *Montrez-moi* (Show me), call out weather phrases in random order, each repeated several times. Pupils select the appropriate card and hold it up to show that they have understood. For increased challenge, include some additional weather types, such as *il gèle* ('it's freezing'), *il y a des nuages* ('it's cloudy') and *il fait mauvais* ('it's horrible weather').
- Small-group or pair work: using the picture cards, pupils question each other, eliciting the appropriate response. Move around the room praising pupils (*Bon travail*, *Bonne prononciation* and so on), which also gives you an opportunity to evaluate the extent to which pupils are beginning to assimilate language.

Plenary

5 minutes

- Pupils collect their picture card sets, and put them into their folders. Monitors collect the folders.
- Remind pupils of the objectives/outcomes and ask whether they have achieved these (thumbs up, thumbs down).
- Ask for volunteers to respond to the learning plenary questions.
- Note engagement with, and responses to, the plenary to inform next steps in teaching and learning.

Lesson 2 *Le temps autour du monde* Weather around the world

Objectives and outcomes
Today we will:
- Learn the names of 12 major French, Belgian and Canadian cities.
- Learn how to create new sentences about the weather in France, Belgium and Canada.
- Practise our speaking and creative writing skills in French.

French to be learned by pupils
à Paris
à Marseille
à Nantes
à Bordeaux
à Lille
à Montpellier
à Nice
au Québec
à Montréal
à Bruxelles
à Bruges
à Charleroi

Resources you will need
- PowerPoint presentation or similar with each of the 12 major cities (see Lesson 2); to enhance the visual aspect of the presentation, include an image from the city. There is a very wide selection of appropriate images online. The presentation should include a random selection of cities matched with a range of weather types, for example *Il fait beau à Lille, Il neige à Montréal, Il pleut à Bruges*
- Set of 12 cards with city names written on them in French (see **Bloomsbury Online Resource 8C**)
- Mini whiteboards or workbooks for written work
- Optional: bilingual vocabulary books and language list sheets

Getting started
5 minutes
- Monitors distribute the sets of both weather pictures and weather words.
- Oral guessing game:
  - Shout out random weather phrases in French; pupils respond by holding up the appropriate picture card.
  - Repeat this step, now shouting out the weather phrases in English for increased challenge; pupils respond by holding up the appropriate weather word card in French.
- Introduce objectives and outcomes, including learning plenary questions, for example:
  - Name as many French, Belgian or Canadian cities as you can in 15 seconds.
  - Tell us the city you'd most like to find out more about, and why.
  - Describe what we did today in French.

- Whole-group discussion in English about major cities across the UK: what are 'capital cities'? Has anyone ever visited any of these cities?
- Whole-group discussion in English about major cities in France/Canada/Belgium: can pupils name any? Has anyone ever visited these cities?
- Note a range of their responses on your whiteboard. Alternatively, select two pupils to be scribes.

Class activities

25 minutes

- Present the 12 major cities, including the name of the country (*en France, au Canada, en Belgique*), each time saying *Voici Paris en France, Voici Toronto au Canada*, etc.
- Pupils repeat each phrase several times; ensure that pupils also have the opportunity to practise saying the word *voici*.
- Practise the phrases using a range of basic questioning techniques, for example:
  - *C'est Paris ou Montréal?*, eliciting the response *C'est ...* Accept the city name alone to differentiate by response.
  - *C'est quelle ville?*
  - *la France, le Canada ou la Belgique?*
- Repeat the presentation of cities, this time including the written name with the appropriate picture.
- Monitors distribute the weather city name cards. Using the instruction *Montrez-moi* (Show me), call out city names in random order, each repeated several times. Pupils select the appropriate card and hold it up to show that they have understood. Vary the questioning by calling out the country. Pupils respond by holding the name card of a city located in that country.
- Small-group or pair work: using all three card sets, demonstrate how to create a whole sentence describing the weather in a city, for example *Il y a du vent à Marseille*. Pupils create a range of sentences and read them out loud to the rest of the class. Where time allows, increase the challenge by encouraging pupils to write down the sentences created by other pupils. Move around the room, praising pupils (*Excellent, Très bien* and so on), which also gives you an opportunity to evaluate the extent to which pupils are beginning to assimilate language.

Plenary

5 minutes

- Pupils collect their picture card sets and put them into their folders. Monitors collect the folders.
- Remind pupils of the objectives/outcomes and ask whether they have achieved these (thumbs up, thumbs down).
- Ask for volunteers to respond to the plenary questions.
- Note engagement with, and responses to, the plenary to inform next steps in teaching and learning.

Lesson 3 *Les couleurs* Colours

Objectives and outcomes

Today we will:
- Learn the words for eight colours in French.
- Discuss the colours of the rainbow, and primary and secondary colours.
- Read a short text about colours in French, and answer some questions about it in our workbooks.

French to be learned by pupils

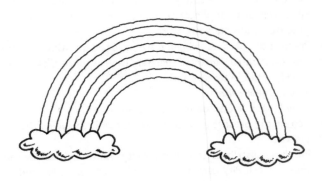

blanc white
bleu blue
brun brown
gris grey
jaune yellow
marron brown
noir black
orange orange
rose pink
rouge red
vert green
violet purple

Select the eight colours you consider to be most appropriate at this point in the children's French learning. If pupils are already confident with French, and have been learning for some time, you may like to introduce more than eight colours.

Resources you will need

- PowerPoint presentation or similar showing a range of colours
- Companion set of colour cards with the colours written on them in French (see **Bloomsbury Online Resource 8D**)
- Photocopied reading text (see **Bloomsbury Online Resource 8E**)
- Optional: bilingual vocabulary books and language list sheets

Getting started

5 minutes
- Rapid Q&A – *Bonjour, ça va?* – between teacher and pupils as well as amongst the pupils themselves to maximise time available for the reading and writing activity.
- Introduce objectives and outcomes, including learning plenary questions, for example:
  - What are the colours of the rainbow in French?
  - Name the primary colours in French.
  - Name the secondary colours in French.
- Give pupils one minute to note as many colours as they can in English on a mini whiteboard, then draw up a list on your whiteboard.
- Select from this list the equivalent colours you will be learning today, ensuring that you have included the colours of the rainbow, and pointing out both primary and secondary colours.

Class activities

25 minutes

- Present your selection of colours, each time saying *C'est rouge, C'est blanc, C'est bleu* etc. Pupils repeat each phrase several times; ensure that pupils also have the opportunity to practise saying the phrase *C'est ...*
- Monitors distribute the colour cards.
- Practise the colours using a range of basic questioning techniques, for example:
  - Multiple choice: *bleu, noir, jaune ...* pupils respond by shouting out the correct colour.
  - *C'est de quelle couleur?*
  - *En anglais, en français*: show a colour indicating which language pupils should respond in; this is best done at high speed.
- Repeat the presentation of colours, this time including the written name with the appropriate picture.
- In English, talk about how rainbows are formed, and identify the colours of the rainbow in French. Reinforce these colours in French by shouting them out several times in random order; pupils demonstrate understanding by holding up the correct colour card. There is an excellent selection of educational video clips online in both English and French on sites such as YouTube, which you may like to screen first if you have any additional time.
- Independent learning: screen the following text (**Bloomsbury Online Resource 8E**) on the whiteboard, and read it out loud to the class. Where time allows, encourage the pupils to read along with you a second time.

  ### Les couleurs

  Salut! Je m'appelle Sophie! J'aime bien les couleurs. J'adore aussi les arcs-en-ciel. Un arc-en-ciel est composé de sept couleurs. Les couleurs sont: rouge, orange, jaune, vert, bleu, indigo et violet. Je connais aussi les couleurs primaires. Elles sont le rouge, le jaune et le bleu. Ma couleur préférée est le vert. Le vert est une couleur secondaire. Le vert est un mélange de bleu et de jaune. Au revoir!

- Monitors distribute the photocopied text and workbooks.
- In their workbooks, pupils respond to the following questions in either English or French according to your differentiation strategy. Questions may also be given in either English or French for further differentiation. Some pupils will find it helpful to be given the questions in both English and French to help them respond in writing in French.
- You can reduce the number of questions where appropriate.
- Encourage pupils where possible to respond in whole sentences, and to give all relevant information. Move around the room praising pupils, and offering additional support and guidance where appropriate.

  Does Sophie like colours?
  What else does she like?
  What are the colours of the rainbow?
  How many primary colours are there?
  Is orange a primary colour?
  What is Sophie's favourite colour?
  What is your favourite colour?
  What are the primary colours you mix to get green?

Est-ce que Sophie aime les couleurs?
Est-ce que Sophie aime les arcs-en-ciel?
Quelles sont les couleurs d'un arc-en-ciel?
Combien de couleurs primaires y a-t-il?
Est l'orange une couleur primaire?
Quelle est la couleur préférée de Sophie?
Quelle est ta couleur préférée?
Oui ou non? Bleu + (plus) jaune = (fait) vert?

- Monitors collect the books, which you can mark and provide feedback on in writing, noting progress and other relevant information.

Plenary
5 minutes
- Remind pupils of the objectives/outcomes and ask whether they have achieved these (thumbs up, thumbs down).
- Ask for volunteers to respond to the AfL plenary questions.
- Note engagement with, and responses to, the plenary to inform next steps in teaching and learning.

Cross-curricular links

English (literacy and oracy): Focus on whole-group, small-group and paired discussion and learning activities, both verbally and in writing.
Science, maths/numeracy and geography: Discuss temperature and climate in a range of countries and regions, including what kinds of foods are cultivated in particular regions. Explore French-speaking countries and regions.
ICT: Keep an eye on the weather across France or other francophone countries during the day using street webcams, for example www.earthtv.com/en/camera-destination/paris-france/.

Further learning opportunities

- Pupils can create an interactive weather chart for the classroom.
- Pupils can read short weather reports describing the weather in various cities or countries and create some of their own.
- Pupils can design and create a rainbow poster, correctly labelled with the colours in French, for classroom display.
- Pupils can update their bilingual vocabulary books, with the support of language list sheets.
- Continue working with colours by exploring world flags.
- Consider introducing items of clothing into following lessons; this works well with both weather and colours, and can lead meaningfully into an introductory engagement with gender agreement.
- Continue to practise creating new sentences with the picture and word cards. Pupils can create new sentences in either French or English for the rest of the class to translate in a team game.

9 *Est-ce que tu as un animal?*
Do you have a pet?

What does the curriculum say?

Pupils should be taught to:
- *Explore the patterns and sounds of language through songs and rhymes and link the spelling, sound and meaning of words.*
- *Speak in sentences, using familiar vocabulary, phrases and basic language structures.*
- *Understand basic grammar appropriate to the language being studied, including (where relevant) feminine, masculine and neuter forms and the conjugation of high-frequency verbs; key features and patterns of the language; how to apply these, for instance, to build sentences; and how these differ from or are similar to English.*

What do I need to know?

These lesson plans suggest ways of teaching pupils how to talk, and write, about pets.

Lesson 1 uses flashcards to introduce ten animals. Flashcard games are a fun, low-tech way of introducing and reinforcing new vocabulary. Hand-drawn pictures, produced either by you, downloaded from the Internet or produced by the children themselves, are very appealing and can be a fun alternative to using PowerPoint. There are some colourful animal flashcards at www.french.ac.nz/pets-and-school-bag.

There is a wide variety of games you can play to introduce new vocabulary, either with flashcards or images on the whiteboard; sequence these carefully in order to gradually reduce the amount of support you give to the pupils. Follow the 'PPP' rule: presentation, practice, production. Initial games should involve pupils simply imitating what you say in a variety of ways; middle section games practise their understanding of the new vocabulary; and the last games require pupils to produce the French words themselves with little, or no, support. If you are using flashcards it is helpful to write the word represented in the picture on the back of the card so that you know what is in the picture without having to turn it around.

Lessons 2 and 3 introduce aspects of grammar: the verb *avoir* (to have) in Lesson 2, and adjectives in Lesson 3. Allow pupils to be creative in choosing and describing their pets: they are allowed to have a tiny dog or an enormous hamster! They could also use the colours introduced in the previous chapter to add to their descriptions.

Comparing English with French

- The question form *Est-ce que tu as un animal?* literally translates as 'Is it that you have an animal?' Many questions in French begin with *Est-ce que ... ?* It can be shortened by beginning with the pronoun, i.e. *Tu as un animal?* Lesson plan 2 focuses on the verb *avoir* (to have). Verb endings in French change according to the pronoun, much as they do in English.
- An 's' on the end of a word, in this case *tu as*, is nearly always silent.
- French has two words for 'you': *tu* is the informal form, which is used for one person who is younger than you or whom you know well; *vous* is the formal or plural form, used for a group of people or with one person whom you do not know well. It is important to choose the correct one as using the incorrect one can cause offence!
- The plural forms of words for pets are formed by adding an 's', just as in English. The exception to this is *oiseau*, which adds an 'x' because it ends with a vowel.
- Most adjectives in French, including colours, follow the noun, rather than precede it, as in English. So, for instance, 'a fast rabbit' is *un lapin rapide*. Two exceptions to this rule feature in Lesson 3: *petit* and *grand*. Both precede the noun.
- The feminine form of adjectives adds an 'e' ending unless the adjective already ends in an 'e'. So *petit* becomes *petite*, *grand* becomes *grande* and *lent* becomes *lente*. The feminine form is determined by the gender of the noun, not the sex of the pet. A big cat called Mimi would therefore be *un grand chat*, even though Mimi is female.

The French you need to teach these lessons

- 10 animal nouns
- How to conjugate the verb *avoir* (to have) (see Lesson 2)
- Question formats: *Est-ce que tu as un animal?/Tu as un animal?* Do you have a pet?
- *les animaux* pets/animals
- *J'adore les animaux* I love animals
- 8 adjectives in masculine and feminine forms
- *fort* loudly
- *doucement* quietly
- quickly *vite*
- slowly *lentement*
- *les filles* girls
- *les garçons* boys
- *C'est ... ou ... ?* Is it ... .or ... .?
- *Numéro un, c'est ... ?* Number one is ... ?
- *Qui a ... ?* Who has ... ?
- *Quel animal a X?* Which animal does X have?
- The different uses of *tu* and *vous*
- *A-t-il un animal?/A-t-elle un animal?* Does he/she have an animal?
- Numbers 1–20

Lesson 1 *Les animaux* Animals

Objectives and outcomes

Today we will:

* Learn how to say the names of 10 pets in French.

French to be learned by pupils

un hamster a hamster
un chat a cat
un chien a dog
un serpent a snake
un poisson a fish
un oiseau bird
un lapin a rabbit
un cochon d'Inde a guinea pig (literally, a pig from India)
une souris a mouse
une tortue a tortoise

Resources you will need

* Photos of your pets/puppet
* 10 pictures of pets, either on flashcards or on the whiteboard
* A French dictionary for pupils who wish to know the French for more exotic pets, e.g. ferret or iguana!

Getting started

5 minutes

* Show pupils photos of your pets, or have the puppet describe his/her pets to the pupils, along the following lines:

  J'adore les animaux. J'ai un chat et un hamster. Mon chat s'appelle Bruno et il a six ans. Mon hamster s'appelle Betty et elle a deux ans.

  Ask pupils to tell you how much they understand, picking out the cognates and drawing on their previous knowledge.

Class activities

25 minutes

* Show pupils ten pictures of pets on flashcards and play the following games. The games are sequenced to allow you to withdraw teacher support gradually, to the point where pupils are able to produce the words independently. Group the words so that you introduce the most accessible first and the most challenging towards the end.
* Show the class one flashcard and ask them to repeat. Add a second flashcard, then go back to the first. Add a third flashcard, then go back to the first and second, and so on.
* On the teacher's command, pupils repeat individual words loudly and quietly, e.g. the teacher shows a picture of a hamster, says *fort*, and the pupils shout *le hamster*; *doucement* and they repeat it quietly.
* Similarly, pupils repeat words slowly (*lentement*) and quickly (*vite*).

- The teacher asks only girls (*les filles*) or only boys (*les garçons*) to repeat, or one side of the classroom, then the other.
- Mexican wave: the teacher divides the class into three groups from left to right and each group repeats part of the phrase, e.g. *J'ai* (first group repeats while standing up and throwing up their arms), *un* (second group), *hamster* (third group). Vary the order, so that the middle group starts first sometimes, then the third group.
- Lip-reading: the teacher picks a flashcard and silently mouths the word. Pupils guess what is on the flashcard.
- The teacher holds up one flashcard and asks: *C'est ... ou ... ?* (Is it ... or ... ?).
- The teacher displays all the flashcards, then removes one and asks which one is missing.
- The teacher reveals one card very slowly.
- The teacher 'flashes' the card to the class.
- The teacher shows the whole pack of flashcards to the group and asks pupils to remember which order they were shown in: *Numéro un, c'est ... ?*
- The teacher hands out flashcards to individuals in the class and instructs them to conceal them. The rest of the class have to either remember who has the card with *le hamster* on it (*Qui a un hamster?*) or name the flashcard that an individual is holding (*Quel animal a Nathan?*).
- Instruct pupils to write up the names of pets or to add drawings of pets to a worksheet showing the words. There are lots of worksheets that can be downloaded from www.primaryresources.co.uk/mfl/mfl_french.htm.

Plenary
5 minutes
- In pairs, one pupil takes it in turns to mime a pet while the other guesses the name.

Lesson 2 *Est-ce que tu as un animal?* Do you have a pet?

Objectives and outcomes
Today we will:
- Learn how to say which pets we have, and how many.

French to be learned by pupils
> *Tu as un animal?* Do you have a pet?
> *avoir* to have
> *j'ai* I have
> *tu as* you have
> *il a* he has
> *elle a* she has
> *nous avons* we have
> *vous avez* you (plural/polite) have
> *ils ont* they (masculine) have
> *elles ont* they (feminine) have

Resources you will need
- Word snake displayed on the whiteboard
- Song lyrics displayed on the whiteboard
- Your best singing voice!

Getting started
5 minutes
- Pupils untangle the word snake on the board, separating out the different animal words:

Chienpoissonchatsourisoiseauserpentcochond'Indehamstertortuelapin

Class activities
20 minutes
- Introduce the following song lyrics on the board, to the tune of the British National Anthem:
> *J'ai un chat, Hannibal* I have a cat, Hannibal
> *Tu as un animal?* Do you have an animal?
> *Elle a un chien* She has a dog
> *Nous avons des poissons* We have some fish
> *Vous avez des lions?* Do you (plural) have any lions?
> *Ils ont deux serpents longs* They have two long snakes
> *J'ai un lapin* I have a rabbit

(Lyrics from *With a Song in my Scheme of Work*, Fawkes, CILT Pathfinder, 1995)

- Explore the meanings of the lyrics with pupils, highlighting the verb *avoir* (to have). Draw comparisons with English to show how the English verb changes too, i.e. 'I *have*', 'he *has*', 'she *has*'. Explain that French has two words for 'you', *tu* and *vous*, and their different uses (see 'Comparing English with French' above).
- Repeat the song lyrics chorally, adding actions to indicate the pronouns:
> *J'ai un chat, Hannibal* – pointing to oneself and making cat's ears on head
> *Tu as un animal?* – pointing to one neighbour

Elle a un chien – pointing to a girl
Nous avons des poissons – pointing to oneself and one other person
Vous avez des lions? – pointing to the whole class
Ils ont deux serpents longs – pointing to two boys
J'ai un lapin – pointing to oneself and jumping out of seat

- Ask the class how they think we say 'he' if *ils* is a group of male pupils. Then ask how we say 'they' if describing a group of girls.
- Pupils write up the song lyrics and illustrate. (Invite them to choose whether they draw stick people to illustrate the pronouns or whether they simply write a translation.)
- Challenge pupils to sing the song without the aid of the written lyrics.

Plenary

5 minutes

- Pupils write up the question *Tu as un animal?* and their answer. They can make this as creative as they like, including numbers, e.g. *J'ai vingt serpents et trois lapins.*
- Ask one pupil the question and when they have given their answer instruct them to ask someone else. Repeat several times, then ask the class, pointing at a boy, *A-t-il un animal?* and, pointing at a girl, *A-t-elle un animal?*, to elicit the use of a sentence using the correct verb form and pronoun.

Lesson 3 *Ton animal est comment?* What's your pet like?

Objectives and outcomes
Today we will:
- Learn how to describe our pets.
- Practise our language detective skills.

French to be learned by pupils
petit small
grand big
énorme enormous
miniscule tiny
drôle funny
timide shy
rapide fast
lent slow
il est he is
elle est she is

Resources you will need
- A list of the eight adjectives above, either displayed on the board or listed on a worksheet for pupils
- Flashcards or images used in Lesson 1.

Getting started
3 minutes
- Word tennis: in pairs, pupils 'bat' the pet nouns backwards and forwards to each other, miming a game of table tennis. They should not repeat what their partner has just said. Model this first with one child.

Class activities
20 minutes
- Introduce the adjectives through mime. Clarify the meanings of the adjectives in English before asking pupils to repeat the mime and the word after you.
- Say the adjective only and ask pupils to mime.
- Reverse roles: now you mime and pupils say the adjective.
- Pupils write up the adjectives, either illustrating with pictures or writing out the words in English.
- Ask pupils what kinds of words they are using to describe pets, i.e. adjectives, and explain that adjectives in French are slightly different to English. Ask them to become language detectives and spot what's different about adjectives in French.
- Invite eight pupils to the front of the class and hand each of them a flashcard with an adjective written on the back, e.g. *un chien timide*. Ask the pupil holding the flashcard to mime the adjective and ask the class *Est-ce que Nathan/Ella a un animal?* to elicit the response *Il a/elle a un chien timide*.
- Ask pupils to spot what's different about the adjective, i.e. the position after the noun.
- Instruct the pupils holding the *souris* and *tortue* cards to mime *grande* and *petite*. Ask pupils what is different about these two adjectives and highlight how these adjectives add an 'e' with feminine nouns and precede the noun, rather than follow it.

Plenary
5 minutes
- Pupils write and illustrate their own sentence in their workbook, framed *J'ai ...* plus pet and adjective. Extension: pupils add the name and age of their pet: *Il s'appelle ... Il a ... ans.*

Cross-curricular links

Literacy: Ask pupils to name examples of other adjectives in English that could be used to describe pets. Who can come up with the longest list?

IT: Visit the following website where pupils can hear the different noises that French animals make and have to drag the animal noise to the correct animal: www.uptoten.com/enfants/boowakwala-world-farms-noises.html. (In French, animals do not make the same sounds as in English!)

Outdoor play: Pupils are put into four teams and choose a French animal noise and a leader. They must find five pictures of animals hidden around the playground. When they find a picture they must make their animal noise to attract the attention of their leader who collects the picture. Only leaders can collect the pictures. Other teams are not allowed to steal a picture another team has found but can make their animal noise to try to attract their leader's attention.

Art: Produce some animal masks that pupils can wear as they introduce themselves to the class, or in an assembly, using animal names and adjectives and describing how animals make different noises in French.

Further learning opportunities

- Pupils modify the *J'ai un chat, Hannibal* song, substituting different pets of their choosing.
- Pupils produce a poster of their pet – real or fictitious – including a photo or picture and a description, with as much information as possible. Encourage them to use colours and numbers too. These can be used in a display.
- Pupils conduct a survey out of school asking family and teachers how many pets they have.
- Play the 'poster game', based on a simple matching game. Paste 20 envelopes onto a large sheet of card, which is displayed on the classroom wall. A number, from 1–20, is written on the front of each envelope in large script. Place into the envelopes 20 small cards with either a word or phrase, e.g. *un lapin/un grand lapin*, or the matching picture. The class is divided into two, three or four teams. The object of the game is for teams to match up the words with the pictures. Each team in turn calls out two numbers and the teacher shows the whole class the cards contained in those envelopes. If the cards match, the teacher removes them and awards the team one point. If they do not match, the teacher replaces the cards and moves on to the next team. Pupils are not allowed to write anything down. If the teacher is feeling generous, the numbers of those envelopes from which cards have been removed can be written up on the board; if not, the pupils have to remember which envelopes are empty! The game is very versatile in that it can be used to reinforce any topic area if you leave it fixed to your classroom wall. It can be a very useful filler activity if you find you have five minutes to spare, and is immensely popular with pupils.

10 *Qu'est-ce que tu aimes faire?* What do you like doing?

What does the curriculum say?

Pupils should be taught to:
- *Explore the patterns and sounds of language through songs and rhymes and link the*
- *spelling, sound and meaning of words.*
- *Develop accurate pronunciation and intonation so that others understand when they are reading aloud or using familiar words and phrases.*
- *Understand and respond to spoken ... language from a variety of authentic sources.*
- *Describe people, places, things and actions orally and in writing.*

What do I need to know?

This chapter looks beyond the school setting. It introduces leisure activities that children take part in outside school, and places to visit in the town.

Lesson 1 introduces hobbies, and the new vocabulary is presented alongside actions to make it more memorable. It is helpful to break down each of the phrases into the constituent words, or syllables of words, to enable pupils to hear each individual component. These are said in time with the action, introducing a memorable rhythm. For instance, to teach *J'aime jouer au tennis*, introduce the phrase as follows: *J'aime* (bounce invisible tennis ball), *jouer* (ditto), *au* (throw tennis ball into the air as if serving), *tennis* (hit the ball). Similarly, *J'aime faire de l'équitation* ('I like horse riding') is a challenging phrase to pronounce and remember, so break the phrase and the word *équitation* down as follows: *J'aime* (first foot in stirrup), *faire* (leg over horse), *de* (pick up reins), *l'équitation* (up and down trotting motion in time with the syllables: l' é-qui-tat-ion). The actions should, as far as possible, match the way the words are said and pupils can be invited to make suggestions. This technique can be used to introduce, and reinforce, all sorts of vocabulary in a fun way, which facilitates pronunciation and memorisation kinaesthetically – the buildings introduced in Lesson 2 of this chapter could be reinforced in this way. Alternatively, the technique can simply be used to revise words that are difficult to pronounce, or pupils' favourite words at the end of the lesson as a plenary activity.

There are many cognates in the French words for buildings in the town, so these should not pose a challenge. The temptation is, however, for pupils to anglicise the pronunciation of these words, so it is worth emphasising the French pronunciation.

Comparing English with French

- The question opening *Qu'est-ce que ... ?* is very common and literally translates as 'What is it that ... ?' It tends to cause problems with pronunciation, as pupils transfer their knowledge of English phonics to French and pronounce the *Qu'est-ce ...* as they would the English word 'question' and the *que* as in 'queen'. *Qu'est-ce* is pronounced 'kess' and *que* 'kuh'.
- The verb 'to like' is *aimer*. Verbs that follow *aimer* are always in the infinitive, i.e. end in *er*, *re* or *ir*, the three types of French verb.
- The French idiom for 'there is/there are ... ' is *il y a ...* , which does not translate literally into English. *Y* is pronounced 'ee'.
- The verb 'to go' is *aller*. When asking for directions, the response to the question *Où est ... ?* ('Where is ... ?') uses the polite imperative form *Allez*.

The French you need to teach these lessons

- The names of 10 hobbies (see Lesson 1)
- *En anglais?* In English?
- *Qu'est-ce que tu aimes faire?* What do you like doing?
- *Levez la main* Put your hand up
- *Qui a 2/3 etc.?* Who's got 2/3 etc.?
- *lentement* slowly
- *vite* quickly
- *fort* loudly
- *doucement* quietly
- *les garçons* boys
- *les filles* girls
- *C'est vrai?* Is that correct?

Lesson 1 *Les passe-temps* Hobbies

Objectives and outcomes
- Today we will learn how to say what you enjoy doing after school and at the weekends.

French to be learned by pupils
J'aime aller au cinéma I like going to the cinema
J'aime danser I like dancing
J'aime jouer de la guitare I like playing the guitar
J'aime lire I like reading
J'aime écouter de la musique I like listening to music
J'aime faire du vélo I like cycling
J'aime faire de l'équitation I like horse riding
J'aime jouer au tennis I like playing tennis
J'aime jouer sur ma tablette I like playing on my tablet
J'aime regarder la télé I like watching TV

Resources you will need
- A list of the ten above hobbies copied onto the board, and the question *Qu'est-ce que tu aimes faire?*
- A means of accessing and showing the BBC Bitesize website

Getting started
5 minutes
- Show pupils a short video from the BBC Bitesize website titled 'My favourite hobby': www.bbc.co.uk/education/clips/zc9m6sg. Ask them to list the hobbies mentioned, in English, after the first viewing. After the second viewing, ask them to note down how the pupils say 'I like' and 'I love'.

Class activities
20 minutes
- Arrange the pupils in a circle, facing inwards. Introduce each of the hobbies with an action that the pupils copy as they repeat the phrase, as outlined above in the Introduction. Ensure that pupils understand what the action represents before they repeat it: *En anglais?*

J'aime lire (turn over the pages of a book)
J'aime danser (dancing)
J'aime jouer de la guitare (strum a guitar)
J'aime écouter de la musique (dance along to music from headphones)
J'aime faire du vélo (pedalling)
J'aime jouer au tennis (serve and hit a tennis ball)
J'aime regarder la télé (draw a square box in the air and peer at it)
J'aime faire de l'équitation (trotting)
J'aime jouer sur ma tablette (move finger around a tablet screen)
J'aime aller au cinéma (eat popcorn and peer at the screen)

- Repeat, varying the order in which they are said.
- Begin saying the phrase and performing the action, and the class completes it.

- Ask individual pupils *Qu'est-ce que tu aimes faire?* The pupil responds with a French phrase, and the action, and the class copies both phrase and action. Encourage pupils to add to the list of the sporting activities covered previously.
- Show pupils the question and list of hobbies on the board. Repeat the question and indicate an answer. Pupils say the phrase, while performing the action.
- Pupils write up the question and their favourite hobby and illustrate it.

Plenary

5 minutes
- Show them the BBC Bitesize video again and ask them to note down in French, if they can, which hobbies are mentioned and whether people like or love them. Can they spot any hobbies that have not yet been covered in the lesson?

Lesson 2 *Ma ville* My town

Objectives and outcomes

Today we will:
- Learn how to describe the places in our town to a French visitor.

French to be learned by pupils

le parc the park
la poste the post office
la banque the bank
la piscine the swimming pool
l'école the school
le cinéma the cinema
la gare the railway station
le supermarché the supermarket
l'église the church
la bibliothèque the library
Qu'est-ce qu'il ya dans ma ville? What is there in my town?
Il y a There is
On y va Let's go

Resources you will need

- 10 photos of the places in your town
- On a display, the question *Qu'est-ce qu'il ya dans ma ville?* and the response *Il y a...*

Getting started

5 minutes
- Instruct pupils to imagine that a French visitor is coming to stay. The visitor could be the puppet/soft toy who has featured in previous lessons. Instruct them to work in pairs to come up with a list, in English, of places in the town that the visitor might like to visit or that they would see if they walked around.

Class activities

20 minutes

- Show the class the images of buildings or places in your town. Ensuring that pupils recognise the buildings in English first, repeat the phrases as a class several times, varying the speed and volume as previously (*lentement, vite, fort, doucement*) and switching between boys and girls.
- Show a picture of a building and ask pupils to repeat after you if you say it correctly and to remain silent if you say it incorrectly. This can become a teacher v. class competition; keep a tally of the score. Alternatively, pupils do a thumbs-up sign if you say the word correctly and thumbs down if you say it incorrectly.
- Present the written question *Qu'est-ce qu'il ya dans ma ville?* Repeat as a class, one word at a time, and then repeat beginning the answer with *Il y a...*
- Note down the name of a building/place in French and challenge pupils to guess which place you're thinking of with the question. You respond with *Oui, il ya ...* or *Non*.
- Pupils repeat the activity in pairs, taking it in turns to note down a place name while their partner guesses.

Plenary

5 minutes

- Sing the '*On y va*' ('Let's go') song to the tune of a football chant, marching, swinging arms and with accompanying actions:

  On y va, on y va, on y va (swinging arms)

  On y va à la piscine (swimming)

  On y va à la bibliothèque (reading)

  On y va à l'église (praying)

Lesson 3 *Où est... ?* Where is... ?

Objectives and outcomes

Today we will:

- Learn how to give directions to a French visitor and to ask for directions yourself.

French to be learned by pupils

  à gauche left

  à droite right

  tout droit straight ahead

  Où est? Where is?

  Allez... Go...

Resources you will need

- Two or three pictures of buildings
- Blindfold (optional)
- Three sets of directions, the word *Allez* and the question *Où est?*, on display
- Copies of a basic map showing pictures of five different buildings on each, and a list of the remaining five buildings, in words, below the map (i.e. two maps, each being an inverse of the other)

Getting started

5 minutes

- Begin with a 'language auction'. Ask pupils who can remember the greatest number of places in the town. Can they think of two? Three? How about five? Give them two minutes to think, and then ask *Qui a deux? Trois?* etc. Whoever claims to remember the highest number is then challenged to list them, beginning with *Il y a...* The rest of the class is tasked with counting them and checking accuracy.

Class activities

20 minutes

- Ask pupils how they would give directions in English. What phrases would they use, i.e. 'Turn left', 'Turn right', 'Go straight on'?
- Introduce the three key phrases and instruct pupils to turn their heads in the direction you give them (*à gauche*, left; *à droite*, right; *tout droit*, straight ahead).
- Introduce the question *Où est...?* ('Where is?') and the response *Allez...* ('Go...').
- Ask for a volunteer to leave the room for a moment, or to close their eyes. Place a picture of a building somewhere in the room. Invite the pupil back into the classroom or to uncover their eyes, tell them which building they're looking for and instruct them to ask in French for directions. Individual pupils in the class direct them to the hidden building, also using French vocabulary. Repeat with a different volunteer.
- Pupils work in pairs to locate buildings on basic maps. Each map (with an identical layout) has five buildings plotted on the map and a further five buildings listed below. Pupil A's map should show the buildings listed only as words on Pupil B's map, and vice versa. Pupils take it in turns to locate the five buildings listed on their map as words by asking their partner for directions, and then mark these on the map. Model this first with an able pupil.

Plenary

5 minutes

- Show the same map on the board with no buildings visible. Invite pupils to direct you to a building. Ask the class to verify whether this is correct: *C'est vrai?* Pupils respond with *Oui* or *Non*.
- Invite individual pupils to the front of the class to take on the role of the teacher for the remaining nine buildings.

Cross-curricular links

Music: www.bbc.co.uk/schools/primarylanguages/french/things_to_do/songs/

Outdoor play: A variation on the 'corners' game is to display four posters on different topics around the playground, e.g. buildings, animals, colours, hobbies. When you blow the whistle, children run to a poster and if theirs is the poster called out they must each say a word related to that topic, or else they are out.

Literacy: Pupils find some additional hobbies in a dictionary. The verb will be listed in the infinitive so they simply need to add *J'aime* before it.

Geography/intercultural understanding: Show pupils photos of buildings in a French town and ask them to compare with the same buildings in this country. What differences do they notice? For example, post boxes in France are yellow, and the letters 'SNCF' for the French national rail company usually appear on French railway stations.

Further learning opportunities

- Pupils suggest other buildings to substitute in the '*On y va*' song or could make up a second verse. The preposition meaning 'to the' with masculine nouns is *au*.
- Play the 'I went to market and bought ... ' game with places in the town. The first pupil says *Dans ma ville il y a une poste*; the second pupil says *Dans ma ville il y a une poste et une banque* and so on.
- Pupils research a French town and produce a poster showing the various buildings that could be incorporated in a display.
- Watch the Teachers' TV *Voici ma ville* film about the capital of Martinique at www.tes.co.uk/teaching-resource/teachers-tv-primary-french–voici-ma-ville-6085165.
- Write a song to the tune of 'When the Saints Go Marching In' to practise building names. The first few lines are

  Qu'est-ce qu'il y a?
  Qu'est-ce qu'il y a?
  Qu'est-ce qu'il y a dans ta ville?
  Il y a une piscine ...
  Et il y a ...

  Pupils produce some shape/emblem poems to illustrate the building names, e.g.

  L'

  é

  L'église

  i

  s

  e

11 *L'heure du conte!* Story time!

What does the curriculum say?

Pupils should be taught to:
- *Listen attentively to spoken language and show understanding by joining in and responding.*
- *Engage in conversations; ask and answer questions; express opinions and respond to those of others.*
- *Speak in sentences, using familiar vocabulary, phrases and basic language structures*
- *Develop accurate pronunciation and intonation so that others understand when they are reading aloud or using familiar words and phrases.*
- *Read carefully and show understanding of words, phrases and simple writing.*
- *Understand basic grammar appropriate to the language being studied, including the conjugation of high-frequency verbs; key features and patterns of the language; how to apply these, for instance, to build sentences; and how these differ from or are similar to English.*
- *Understand and respond to spoken and written language from a variety of authentic sources.*

In further learning opportunities, pupils could be taught to:
- *Write phrases from memory, and adapt these to create new sentences, to express ideas clearly.*
- *Broaden their vocabulary and develop their ability to understand new words that are introduced into familiar written material, including through using a dictionary.*

Teachers should aim to:
- *Foster pupils' curiosity and deepen their understanding of the world.*

What do I need to know?

Children respond enthusiastically to stories and there are many stories that are perfect for the primary French classroom. They provide the opportunity to engage with rich language, moving beyond single sentences, and thereby creating meaningful links between English and the development of general literacy skills, and learning in French. Stories enable children to work with all four skills, and to think about how language works. Choosing a story with which children are already familiar is a good place to start, as we saw in Chapter 7, *C'est bon pour la santé*, for example, with ideas for cross-curricular learning using 'The Very Hungry Caterpillar' ('*La chenille qui fait des trous*') or 'Go Away Big Green Monster' ('*Va t'en grand monstre vert*'). This chapter uses 'Jack and the Beanstalk' ('*Jacques et le haricot magique*') to get us started with storytelling in French, and also provides a good opportunity to revisit the French words for family members we looked at in Chapter 3. In 'Further learning opportunities' there are ideas for building on language we looked at in Chapter 9, *Est-ce que tu as un animal?*, moving from domestic to farm animals, and writing creatively using the nursery rhyme 'The Farmer's in his Den' as a writing frame. A list of stories that work well in the primary French classroom is given at the end of the chapter.

Lesson 1 introduces pupils to the story of 'Jack and the Beanstalk', *Jacques et le haricot magique*, with a focus on developing listening and reading skills in French.

Lesson 2 engages pupils more closely with the story, with a particular focus on verbs.

Lesson 3 gives pupils the opportunity to build the story in French, to read out loud 'in the round' and to have a go at translating!

Additional notes

The chapter takes as its focal point the story resource for 'Jack and the Beanstalk', created by the Qualification and Curriculum Authority (QCA), the Teacher Development Agency (TDA) and the Languages team at the National Centre for Languages (CILT). Though these agencies are no longer operating, many of their resources are still available online. The full text for the story is given on the following page; it may look like a lot of 'new' language, but in reality, most of it will be familiar. The story follows the traditional structure of storytelling, and uses repetition to create the narrative. You will see too that many words are either ones we've already looked at in the book, such as *marché* (market), or cognates or near cognates, such as *arriver* (to arrive) and *le géant* (giant). Watch the film clip yourself several times prior to this series of lessons to help you develop accurate pronunciation and to familiarise yourself with the range of French used in the story.

Jacques et le haricot magique

Hum! Hum! Hum! Hum!

Voici l'histoire... d'un garçon.

Bonjour! Comment t'appelles-tu?
Je m'appelle Jacques.

Jacques est pauvre... Maman est pauvre...
Jacques et Maman deviennent de plus en plus pauvres... de plus en plus pauvres.

Rien pour le petit déjeuner...
Rien pour le déjeuner...
Rien pour le dîner...
Rien du tout!

Alors, Maman dit:

« Jacques, vendons la vache. »
Meuh! Meuh! Meuh! Meuh! Meuh!

« Va au marché. Vite! Vite! »

Jacques et la vache vont au marché.
Ils rencontrent un vieil homme.
« Je voidrais acheter une vache.
Voici cinq haricots magiques.
Un... deux... trois...
quatre... cinq... »

Mais Maman dit :
« Que tu es bête! »
Elle prend les haricots... les haricots magiques...
Un... deux... trois...
quatre... cinq...

Et elle les jete!

Mais la nuit, une tige de haricot magique pousse.
Elle pousse... Elle pousse... Elle pousse...
Whoosh!

Jacques grimpe à la tige de haricot magique.
Il grimpe... il grimpe... il grimpe... jusqu'au ciel.

Jacques voit un château géant.
Toc... toc... toc... toc...
toc... personne!

Jacques entre dans le château.
Il voit des pièces d'or, une poule et une harpe magique.

Le géant arrive!
Le grand, grand géant!
Cache-toi, Jacques!
« Hum! Hum! Hum! Hum!
Ça sent le garçon! »
Mais il ne trouve pas Jacques.

Le géant dort.
RRRRRRRRRRRRRRRRRRR
Jacques entre à pas de loup.
Il prend les pièces d'or.

Jacques glisse le long de la tige...
il glisse... il glisse... il glisse...
Et après?

Jacques grimpe à la tige de haricot magique.
Il grimpe... il grimpe... il grimpe... jusqu'au ciel.
Et Jacque entre dans le château...
Et il voit... la poule... et la harpe magique.

Le géant arrive!

Le grand, grand géant!
Cache-toi, Jacques!
« Hum! Hum! Hum! Hum!
Ça sent le garçon! » Mais il ne trouve pas Jacques.

Le géant dort.
RRRRRRRRRRRRRRRRRRR
Jacques entre à pas de loup.
Il prend la poule.

Jacques glisse le long de la tige...
il glisse... il glisse... il glisse...
Et après?

Jacques grimpe à la tige de haricot magique.
Il grimpe... il grimpe... il grimpe... jusqu'au ciel.
Et Jacque entre dans le château...
Et il voit... la harpe magique.

Le géant arrive!
Le grand, grand géant!
Cache-toi, Jacques!
« Hum! Hum! Hum! Hum!
Ça sent le garçon! » Mais il ne trouve pas Jacques.

Le géant dort.
RRRRRRRRRRRRRRRRRRR
Jacques entre à pas de loup.
Il prend la harpe magique.

Mais le géant se réveille!
Le géant chasse Jacques.
Jacques glisse le long de la tige...
il glisse... il glisse... il glisse...
Mais le géant vient aussi!

Jacques cherche une hache!
Vite! Vite!
Jacques abat la tige de haricot.
Vite! Vite!
PATATRAS!
Et le géant tombe...
PATATRAS!
Et ça, c'est la fin du géant.
Et ça, c'est la fin de l'histoire

Jacques et le haricot magique, based on 'Jack and the Beanstalk', by the Qualification and Curriculum Authority (QCA), the Teacher Development Agency (TDA) and the National Centre for Languages (CILT).

Comparing English with French

- The title of the story 'Jack and the Beanstalk' is slightly different in French: it translates as 'Jack and the Magic Bean'.
- Title nouns are not necessarily capitalised in French as they are in English.
- The phrase 'Once upon a time … ' signposts to children that a story is about to begin; the story is generally related in the past tense. This is similar to the phrases *Il était une fois* or *Un jour …* so using the present tense is not strictly 'correct'; however, I have always used the phrases in French to communicate to pupils that it's story time!
- The infinitive of English verbs always begins with 'to … ': 'to say', 'to arrive', 'to be', 'to do' and so on. French verbs do not use this pattern, and the infinitive is indicated by the ending, for example *dire*, *arriver* and *dormir*.

The French you need to teach these lessons

- *Jacques et le haricot magique* Jack and the Beanstalk
- *Dans mon sac j'ai…* In my bag I have…
- *l 'infinitif* the infinitive
- *les verbes* verbs (you will not have to know how to conjugate these fully, or know them all off by heart; the aim of Lesson 2 is to encourage pupils to recognise the place and function of verbs in a sentence, so the verbs are listed as a reference, and you can select which ones to focus on):

s'appeler to be called	*être* to be
est is	*devenir* to become
ils/elles deviennent they become	*dire* to say
dit says	*vendre* to sell
vendons let's sell	*aller* to go
va goes	*ils/elles vont* they go
rencontrer to meet	*ils/elles rencontrent* they meet
vouloir to want	*je voudrais* I would like
prendre to take	*prend* takes
jeter to throw	*jette* throws
grimper to climb	*grimpe* climbs
voir to see	*voit* sees
entrer to enter, go into	*entre* enters, goes into
arriver to arrive	*arrive* arrives
dormir to sleep	*dort* sleeps
glisser to slide	*glisse* slides
trouver to find	*trouve* finds
se réveiller to wake up	*se réveille* wakes up
chasser to chase	*chasse* chases
venir to come	*vient* comes
chercher to look for	*cherche* looks for
abattre to cut down	*abat* cuts down
tomber to fall	*tombe* falls

Lesson 1 *Jacques et le haricot magique* Jack and the Beanstalk

Objectives and outcomes
Today we will:
- Revise our words for fruit and vegetables in French.
- Discuss the story of 'Jack and the Beanstalk' in English.
- Listen to and read the story of 'Jack and the Beanstalk' in French.

French to be learned by pupils
- The learning purpose of this introductory lesson to 'Jack and the Beanstalk' is to engage with a longer text in French, using a range of language learning strategies (for example, look for cognates, use pictures and repeated phrases to deduce meaning) as well as their understanding and knowledge of the story in English to follow it in French. Therefore Lesson 1 does not specify a particular range of words to learn explicitly.

Resources you will need
- Plastic fruit or pictures of fruit with a small bag/basket
- Access to, and capacity to screen, the film of 'Jack and the Beanstalk' on YouTube: www.youtube.com/watch?v=A3nImgZAtjM.

Getting started
5 minutes
- Introduce objectives and outcomes.
- Play the game *Dans mon sac j'ai...* ('In my bag I have...'). This is a guessing game for oral recap of language. Show all the items in the bag, and very quickly run through the French words for them, then put them all into the bag. Holding an item within the bag so that they can't see it, say *Dans mon sac j'ai...* and pupils guess what you are holding. This works well for team games too. For additional challenge, hold two items, one in each hand, and pupils are required to give the response using a conjunction (and/*et*).

Class activities
20 minutes
- Show your symbol to indicate that you will be using English for communication.
- Engage pupils in a discussion about the story of 'Jack and the Beanstalk'; can they retell the story as a group in English? They may need some gentle prompting according to their age; discussion and debate can address higher-level thinking, such as:
  - Discuss what they consider to be the point or moral of the story.
  - Was *Maman*'s decision to sell the cow at market the right one?
  - Why do you think that?
  - If you were Jacques, would you have sold the cow to a stranger for five beans? Why/why not?
  - Is it a good idea to go into houses uninvited?
  - Do you think Jacques is a thief? Why/why not?
  - Who is the hero of the story? Why?
  - Is the giant a 'villain'? Why/why not?

- Screen the film of 'Jack and the Beanstalk'. You can either screen it in its entirety or pause at strategic points to check for understanding, to practise pronunciation or to prompt pupils to identify words they already know. This also works well for a mini translation activity.
- Screen the story a second time, encouraging pupils to read aloud along with the narrator; the text is given in subtitles throughout the story.

Plenary
5 minutes
- Call out a range of individual words and phrases in French from the story, asking *En anglais?* This is a simple yet very effective way of assessing initial understanding.
- Remind pupils of the objectives/outcomes and ask whether they have achieved these.

Lesson 2 *Les verbes français* Fun with French verbs

Objectives and outcomes
Today we will:
- Continue working on our French story *Jacques et le haricot magique*.
- Learn to recognise and say six French verbs.

French to be learned by pupils
être/je suis to be/I am
aller/je vais to go/I go (I am going)
vouloir/je voudrais to want/I would like
arriver/j'arrive to arrive/I arrive
se réveiller/je me réveille to wake up/I wake up
dire/je dis to say/I say
Optional: choose additional verbs from the selection above if appropriate to your year group.

Additional learning content
Discussion of grammar terminology and comparison with English – infinitive, conjugation.

Resources you will need
- PowerPoint or similar presentation featuring the six verbs in written form above, preferably with an image to illustrate the action. These should initially be shown in English only. The subsequent slides should show both the infinitive form and the first person singular in French, and you can repeat the English equivalent for additional support. You may consider it more appropriate to omit the infinitive form and focus on the first person singular at this stage, depending on the age and stage of the pupils you are working with
- Between 10 and 20 slides with a range of verbs and words from the story appearing in both English and French, for the plenary activity
- Worksheet with the text reproduced. Use varying sections of the text for learners; for example, some learners will be able to engage with the entire text, whilst others may find it too challenging, which can demotivate children very quickly. Providing parallel columns with the French and English text in each is a successful scaffolding strategy, so you may like to create a worksheet in that structure

- Highlighter pens for pupils (any colour)
- Children's vocabulary books

Getting started

5 minutes

- Introduce objectives and outcomes.
- Repeat the plenary activity from Lesson I as the starter: call out a range of individual words and phrases in French from the story, asking *En anglais?* Increase the challenge by including some words/phrases in English, asking *En français?*

Class activities

20 minutes

- Read the story in French out loud to refresh pupils' memories.
- Indicate that you will now be using English; elicit pupils' understanding of verbs, their purpose, how they work and so on.
- Screen the initial slides showing the verbs in English to facilitate this discussion.
- Now work through the slides with the French verbs; pupils repeat, focusing on good pronunciation. Use a range of yes/no/true/false/picture question forms to practise; ensure that pupils use the personal pronoun *je*.
- Distribute the worksheet with the text (or sections from it) reproduced. Pupils should work in pairs; explain that they will read their text together, underlining the verbs they recognise, and highlighting in the colour you have selected words that they think are also verbs.
- As they work, move around the learning pairs to offer support and guidance; this will also give you the chance to informally assess children's learning.
- Whole-group discussion of worksheet activity, identifying verbs.
- Pupils write their new verbs in their vocabulary books.

Plenary

5 minutes

- Screen the final slides for a memory game of key words and phrases from the story, and the six verbs in the infinitive form (where you have used it) and conjugated in the first person singular. This is best done at high speed, in small teams, with points awarded for each correct response.
- Remind pupils of the objectives/outcomes and ask whether they have achieved these.

Lesson 3 *Lisons ensemble* Reading together

Objectives and outcomes

Today we will:

- Build the story of 'Jack and the Beanstalk' in French
- Do some French translation!
- Read out loud in our best French accents

French to be learned by pupils

- Lesson 3 is conceptualised as a skills development and confidence-building opportunity: pupils are able to revisit words, phrases and concepts in a whole-group, cooperative context, thus the focus is on words addressed explicitly in Lesson 2, and implicitly in both Lessons 1 and 2, within the narrative of the story.

Resources you will need

- Sets of matching text cards, with extracts from the story in English and French for the matching mini-translation activity
- 'Build the story' resource: story text in separate story strips or boards for pupils to reconstruct, one set for each learning group; differentiate simply yet effectively by varying the amount of text on each card
- Simple flashcards with a range of words/phrases written on them in French for the plenary activity
- Access to, and capacity for screening of, the *Jacques et le haricot magique* online film if required

Getting started

5 minutes

- Introduce objectives and outcomes.
- Play 'Shout it Out'! Pupils shout out as many words or phrases in French from the previous two lessons as they can remember. A variation of this game is to have two teams: remember to let children choose a name for their team, or allocate a name, for example: *Équipe Un s'appelle les haricots verts, Équipe Deux s'appelle les géants*; one team shouts out in either French or English, the other wins a point if they respond appropriately. To ensure that all children can participate fully, you can provide reference sheets, or give them 60 seconds to look quickly at their vocabulary books.

Class activities

20 minutes

- If you think it necessary, screen the film clip again, encouraging pupils to read out loud along with the narrator.
- Monitors distribute the mini translation card sets, in pairs or small groups.
- In pairs or small groups, pupils match the French and English words, phrases and sentences from the story.
- For additional challenge, you can include 'new' sentences, using the language covered in other contexts.
- Whole-group discussion of translation activity. This also works well continuing as a team game: each team is required to read out what they consider to be the correct translation from the cards you read out. Read out in French first, they offer the English, then vice versa.
- Monitors distribute the 'build the story' sets. Explain that the goal of the game is to reconstruct the story of 'Jack and the Beanstalk'. Be specific about the amount of time available; this can

vary according to the class you are working with. You might prefer to nominate learning groups yourself, as this can ensure a more successful differentiated learning experience.

- Select a group to read their story out loud to the class; taking it in turns, each pupil in the group reads a sentence out loud.
- As each sentence is read out loud, the other groups offer an English translation.

Plenary
5 minutes

- Play '*chaud ou froid*' ('hot or cold'). Ask for a volunteer. The volunteer stands outside the classroom for a couple of seconds while you and the rest of the class decide where to hide the flashcard. The pupil enters and starts to hunt for the flashcard, with the rest of the class calling *chaud* or *froid* as the pupil either gets near to, or moves away from, the hiding place. When the pupil finds the card, he/she reads the French word/phrase/sentence out loud in his/her best French accent, and for a bonus point gives the English translation. This is very popular game, so you might like to give the lesson a little additional time to enable you to play it several times! Instead of using *chaud/froid*, you can use specific phrases, getting increasingly louder or lower as the pupil approaches or moves away from the hiding place; a perfect one here would be *Jacques et le haricot magique*.
- Remind pupils of the objectives/outcomes and ask whether they have achieved these.

Cross-curricular links

English:
- Rewrite the story with a series of alternative events and endings.
- Create new characters.
- Create a storyboard (linking also with **art and design**).

Art and design/ICT:
- Design your own book cover (and marketing information, linking again with literacy, i.e. writing for specific purposes).
- Design costumes for the individual characters, including the animals!
- Search on Amazon or a similar online bookseller for 'Jack and the Beanstalk' book covers. Which of these do you prefer, and why?
- Save the covers as JPEGs, and create posters in publishing software advertising the book, being creative with WordArt, fonts, drop caps, watermarks and other design features.
- Mind-map display ideas, choose a display design as a group and create it over a series of lessons.

Drama:
- Recreate the story as a play for performance to the school/parents.
- In small groups, choose a particular point in the story and mime it; the rest of the group have to work out what part of the story it is. Or ask them what happens immediately before, or immediately after.

Science: Planting and growing vegetables; life cycles; healthy eating (aligning with Chapter 7); animals and their role in the food chain.

Citizenship: Discussion about individual responsibility; empathising with others; behaving fairly and justly; respect for others and their belongings; understanding issues related to economic well-being.

Cultural traditions and ways of living: Harvest Festival; living in rural communities.

Further learning opportunities

- Children enjoy exploring stories from around the world, and they offer a meaningful insight into the lives of other children too. www.worldstories.org.uk/stories/stories has an enormous range of stories that you can browse through in a range of languages. The level of French in some of the stories (for example 'Goldilocks and the Three Bears' and 'Sleeping Beauty') is too advanced for the primary classroom, but where the focus is on developing cultural understanding, the stories in English are really useful.
- World Book Day, which takes places annually in March, is a great opportunity to align learning in English and in French: http://worldbookday.com/.
- Similarly, National Poetry Day, which generally takes place in October, is an excellent vehicle for exploring both English and French poetry or traditional nursery rhymes.
- Looking at farm animals, and building on language learned in Chapter 9, 'Do you have a pet?' links nicely with the series of lessons on 'Jack and the Beanstalk'. Using the nursery rhyme 'The Farmer's in his Den' ('Le fermier dans son pré'), you can practise family members and domestic animals, and create new versions to include a range of farm animals too. Pupils will be familiar with the routine of creative composing from their work in Chapter 7. Try this film, which includes the lyrics as subtitles; the melody works slightly differently in parts, so rehearse it first! www.youtube.com/watch?v=I2UXqfi7Rqg
- Begin to work with the 'you' form of the verbs addressed in Lesson 3, as this develops and progresses children's understanding and knowledge of French verbs.

Stories that work well in the primary French classroom

Here are some suggestions for other suitable stories you may like to try with your pupils; a quick online search will give you many very good versions and resources in a variety of formats:
- *Le petit chaperon rouge* 'Little Red Riding Hood'
- *Les trois petits cochons* 'The Three Little Pigs'
- *Le navet géant/énorme* 'The Enormous Turnip'
- *Roule galette* 'The Gingerbread Man' (the story is not quite the same, but shares sufficient similarities to work well, and is very popular with children)
- *Boucle d'or et les trois ours* 'Goldilocks and the Three Bears'
- *Cendrillon* 'Cinderella'
- *Blanche-Neige et les sept nains* 'Snow White and the Seven Dwarfs'
- Try also the 'Little Brown Bear' series: *Petit ours brun*. These are authentic French books, widely available via online booksellers, and perfect for the primary French classroom.

Recommended resources

Websites, blogs & Tweeters

You can download lesson plans, worksheets, PowerPoint presentations and activities from the following websites. Some of the lesson plans in the book direct you to specific websites for resources.

Online resources and documentation

CfBT Education Trust (2015) *Language Trends 2014/15*
DFE (2013) *Languages Programmes of Study Key Stage 2*, National Curriculum in England
www.thelivelylanguagescompany.net – information, resources, policy and curriculum documentation
http://lightbulblanguages.co.uk/resources-primary.htm – schemes of work, podcasts, and resources
www.teachingideas.co.uk/subjects/languages – free posters, banners, learning mats and worksheets to download
www.primaryresources.co.uk/mfl/mfl.htm – PowerPoint presentations, games and worksheets
www.tes.com/primary-teaching-resources – quizzes, self-assessment charts, games and worksheets
www.bbc.co.uk/schools/primarylanguages/french/ – audio clips, songs and photos arranged by topic
www.tes.com/teachers-tv-primary-french-lesson-starters – short videos covering a range of topics and giving some insight into French culture
http://lightbulblanguages.blogspot.co.uk/ - KS1 and 2 resources for games and activities
http://primarygamesarena.com/Play/French-vocabulary-2139 – games and audio models
Language Trends 2014/15, *The state of language learning in primary and secondary schools in England* (2015), CfBT Education Trust
National Languages Strategy (2002), *Languages for All: Languages for Life*, DfES

Social media

Twitter:
#primarymfl
@LivelyLangs
@LightBulbLangs
@VB_PrimaryLang

French subject knowledge development and enhancement

Duolingo: Free web-based language learning, www.duolingo.com
McLachlan, A. (2010) *French for Primary School Teachers Pack: Teach Yourself*, London: Hodder and Stoughton
www.open.edu/openlearn/ – free online courses from the Open University

Further reading

Focus on practice

Bourdais, D. and Finnie, S (2015) *Games for Teaching Primary French*, Carmarthen: Crown House Publishing

Cave, S. (2006) *100+ Fun Ideas for Practising Modern Foreign Languages in the Primary Classroom: Activities for Developing Oracy and Literacy Skills*, Bedfordshire: Brilliant Publications

Chadwick, S. and MacGregor, H. (2004) *Singing French (book and CD): 22 Photocopiable Songs and Chants for Learning French*, London: Bloomsbury

Cheater, C. and Farren, A. (2001) *The Literacy Link*, Young Pathfinder 9, London: CILT

Drinkwater, N. (2008) *Classroom Gems: Games and Activities for Primary Modern Foreign Languages*, Harlow: Pearson Education

Jones, J. and Coffey, S. (2013) *Modern Foreign Languages 5–11*, 2nd edn., Abingdon: Routledge

Jones, J. and McLachlan, A. (2009) *Primary Languages in Practice: A Guide to Teaching and Learning*, Berkshire: Open University Press

Kirsch, C. (2008) *Teaching Foreign Languages in the Primary School*, London: Bloomsbury

Watts, C, and Phillips, H. (2015) *Bringing French to Life: Creative Activities for 5–11*, Abingdon: Routledge

Focus on research

Bevis, R. and Gregory, A. (2005) *Mind the Gap! Improving Transition between Key Stage 2 and 3*, London: CILT

Blondin, C. et al. (1998) *Foreign Languages in Primary and Pre-School Education*, London: CILT

Driscoll, P. and Frost, D. (eds) (1999) *The Teaching of Modern Foreign Languages in the Primary School*, London: Routledge

Edelenbos, P. and Johnstone, R. (1996) *Researching Languages at Primary School. Some European Perspectives*, London: CILT

Language Learning Journal, 37 (2) July 2009 (special issue 1 on foreign languages in primary schools)

Language Learning Journal, 38 (2) July 2010 (special issue 2 on foreign languages in primary schools)

Martin, C. (2000), *An Analysis of National and International Research on the Provision of Modern Foreign Languages in Primary Schools*, Qualifications and Curriculum Authority

National Languages Strategy (2002), Languages for All: Languages for Life, DfES

Nuffield Languages Inquiry (2000), *Languages: The Next Generation*, London: The Nuffield Foundation

Sharpe, K. (2001), *Modern Foreign Languages in the Primary School – The What, Why and How of Early MFL Teaching*, London: Kogan Page